Success with

Indoor Ferns

SUSANNE AMBERGER-OCHSENBAUER

Series Editor:
LESLEY YOUNG

Introduction

Anyone can have luxuriant green foliage in their living room all year round. Our great grandparents knew this and stocked their parlors with many splendid types of ferns. Ever since, these exotic evergreen plants with their elegant palm-frond leaves have been listed among the most popular indoor plants of all. Unfortunately, what could be a wonderful display is often ruined as the wrong position and mistakes in care soon cause ferns to turn yellow and dry up.

In this guide, Susanne Amberger-Ochsenbauer, an experienced ornamental plant gardener, will show you how to care for tropical ferns according to the requirements of the individual species so that they will flourish for a long time, even when grown under less favorable conditions. Simple step-by-step instructions and numerous color illustrations are used to demonstrate all that you need to know about the care of ferns and to prove the immense variety of these decorative plants, as well as to explain their astonishing methods of reproduction. The beautiful color photographs specially taken for this book will introduce you to the most popular indoor ferns along with some rarities for both beginner and expert to enjoy.

Contents

Pellaea falcata.

Cyrtomium with clusters of spores.

Young leaves of Asplenium antiguum in the process of unfurling.

The author
Dr Susanne Amberger-Ochsenbauer is an agricultural engineer who specializes in gardening with an emphasis on ornamental plants. She is also a scientific researcher at the Institute for Soil Research and Plant Nutrition at the Fachhochschule Weihenstephan and the author of numerous publications.
NB: Please read the Author's notes on page 62 so that your enjoyment of indoor ferns may not be impaired.

Living fossils

Spore pattern.

Mention the word "fern" and it conjures up a vision of lovely shades of green, fine, feathery fronds and elegant leaves. Quite apart from this image, this fascinating class of plants, which today numbers some 9,500 different species, holds a number of other surprises for the interested plant lover.

Relics from the carboniferous era

The evolution of fern plants began as far back as 400 million years ago in the earliest periods of Earth's history, long before the rise of seed-bearing plants. Ferns were at their most abundant during the carboniferous era when gigantic forests of tree-sized ferns and mare's tail plants covered the planet. They played a major role in the formation of our present-day coalfields. The visible proof of this is the many fossil ferns which are constantly found and which allow a continuing investigation of the vegetation of the carboniferous period. The development of ferns coincides with a very interesting phase of evolution. During this time, lifeforms that originally lived in the seas were beginning to colonize dry land. Within the plant world this development coincided with the appearance of mosses and ferns. Ferns, therefore, including ancient fossil ferns as well as *Lycopodia* and mare's tail species, can truly be said to belong among the most ancient higher terrestrial plants.

Life in the most varied types of climate

Steady temperatures, shade and high humidity, which constitute the typical climatic conditions of a rain forest, are often considered to be the ideal conditions in which to grow ferns and for most of the indoor ferns derived from tropical regions this does apply. One should not forget, however, that ferns occur all over the world. Just think of the indigenous European species, like lady fern (*Athyrium filix-femina*), male fern (*Dryopteris filix-mas*), or hard fern (*Blechnum spicant*).
Ferns will also colonize areas where you would never expect to find representatives of this plant group. Different species are distributed as far as sub-arctic regions, for example maidenhair spleenwort (*Asplenium trichomanes*) or *Adiantum pedatum*. Others are found growing in particularly exposed positions on rocks, for example, *Ceterach officinarum*. Even in regions with hot, dry seasons, you will still find ferns like *Davallia denticulata* which manages to survive the periods after its leaves have dried up by forming rhizomes. Exactly the opposite type of arrangement has been adopted by floating ferns like *Salvinia* or *Azolla* which live on the surface of water.

Firmly anchored in the ground or high in the air

The indigenous European ferns grow either on the ground (terrestrial) or in trees (epiphytic).
The ground dwellers often occur along the banks of streams or rivers, around springs, and among rocks (see p. 5). This shows that they prefer moist, though not wet, positions that are characterized by high humidity and slightly filtered light, important indicators as to the kind of care they require when indoors. One example is maidenhair fern (*Adiantum*).
The epiphytes colonize tree trunks and the forks of branches (see p. 5) and therefore can manage with very little soil or compost. They require conditions of high humidity and frequent rainfall to supply their water and nutrients. This elevated position also ensures that they receive adequate light, even in a tropical rain forest, another factor which needs to be taken into account when caring for them. Examples include staghorn ferns (*Platycerium*) and bird's-nest fern (*Asplenium nidus*). Both species have evolved funnel-like leaves that are able to catch falling twigs and leaves which, over a period of time, will develop into a little pocket of humus. Epiphytes can also be grown in pots but you will have to make quite sure they are in very loose, coarse compost. Some types of fern can grow both as terrestrials or as epiphytes and

Bird's nest fern (Asplenium) growing as an epiphyte and collecting humus in its rosette.

...us prove to be very flexible with ...spect to their position. Among ...ese are included many sword fern ...ecies (*Nephrolepis*).

An astonishing variety of ...hapes

...erns do not produce any flowers ...ut they more than make up for this ...ck with their enormous range of ...fferent shapes of growth and ...aves.

...he shapes of growth are so many ...at this alone makes it possible to ...roduce countless variety when

growing ferns as indoor plants. Ferns grow:

● upright, like *Arachniodes adiantiformis*

● elegantly drooping, like maidenhair fern (*Adiantum*)

● hanging, like *Adiantum caudatum* which is excellent for hanging containers, epiphyte trunks, or for creating a fern pillar

● climbing, like *Lygodium* which can be trained up sticks or posts (see p. 56)

● tree-like, like several types of hard fern (*Blechnum*) which form

Hart's-tongue fern (*Phyllitis scolopendrium*) is a terrestrial fern that is indigenous to northern Europe.

small trunks in old age, not to mention the huge tree ferns whose trunks can grow to a height of 67 ft (20 m).

The shapes of the leaves also show a great range of different forms and variations (see pp. 10-11). Besides the classic palm-frond-shaped leaves, as displayed by species of *Nephrolepis*, there are the undivided leaves of bird's-nest fern (*Asplenium nidis* or *Asplenium antiguum*) and of many other species. In direct contrast, you can also find very finely feathered leaves, as with individual forms of maidenhair fern (*Adiantum*) or sword fern (*Nephrolepis*).

The plants of some genera develop two kinds of leaves. This is called heterophyllia. First, young leaves develop which usually have wider fronds (see p. 7) and shorter leaf stalks. They have no spores (see p. 7) and are, therefore, sterile. With increasing maturity, the plant later produces spore-bearing, fertile fronds, often on longer stalks, as with ribbon fern (*Pteris*), and which stand stiffly upright and possess many narrow fronds, as with hard fern (*Blechnum*). Among other genera, like royal fern (*Osmunda*), which are grown as outdoor plants, special fronds are produced which bear spore capsules.

The arrangement of spore capsules (see pp. 8-9) on the leaf undersides is also very varied and can be an important distinguishing feature in determining the species of a plant. The spore capsules may be grouped together in round, long, kidney-shaped, urn-shaped, or striped formations. These are called sori (see pp. 8-9).

Ferns are not only green

By appearing in all shades of green, ferns more than make up for their lack of brightly colored flowers. If you look at them a little closer than most people do, however, you will also discover a discreet and surprising variety of colors among the plants themselves.

Leaves and stalks: The most conspicuous are variegated, patterned in green-white, green-yellow, or green-red, and often with striped fronds. Sometimes the young leaves will be light green or reddish when shooting. The spectrum of colors on stalks can range from yellow to green and brown to black. Either the stalks themselves will display these colors or they will bear brown, sometimes even silvery, scales.

Rhizomes: Some ferns produce creeping rhizomes, either below or above ground (see p. 7), that may be covered in whitish, yellow, golden brown, or red brown scales which make an interesting, eye-catching spectacle.

Sori and spores: The groupings of spores on the undersides of leaves may also be quite attractive. These sori are often creamy white in their unripe state and change color to become brown when they are mature. Different species possess conspicuously colored spore capsules; for example, *Phlebodium aureum*. This fern is known for its round, golden yellow clusters of spores. Black stripes made up of lines of spores create interesting contrasts on white and green striped fronds as formed by many species of ribbon fern (*Pteris*). In the case of *Pteris cretica* "Albolineata," these parts of the plant are like graphic works of art. The spores themselves are black, brown, gray, or yellow, but even ferns with green spores are known, for example *Platycerium wallichii*.

Fertilization

Ferns do not form flowers and seed but they still manage to reproduce. Reproduction proceeds through two completely separate phases termed "alternating generations" (see p. 8). During the non-sexual phase, spores are formed on the undersides of the fern fronds. The spores germinate and produce a prothallus which, in turn, forms male and female sexual organs on its under side, which then begin a sexual phase. Provided conditions are favorable, this is the phase when fertilization takes place and a new fern plant is created.

How ferns became fashionable

There is evidence from as early as the first half of the seventeenth century that ferns were being cultivated in Europe. The tropical ferns often grown today were mostly introduced to Europe from the end of the eighteenth to the middle of the nineteenth century. They were often transported in a special glass box called a Wardian case, invented by a British doctor named Nathaniel Ward. This sealed glass tank can be seen as the forerunner of the bottle garden (see p. 21) and various indoor glass display cases. Glass cases and enclosed plant picture windows were very popular in the second half of the nineteenth century and enabled the successful cultivation of ferns, orchids, and other tropical plants. In keeping with the prevailing fashion of the time, large elaborately decorated containers were constructed to grace the salons of the wealthy middle and upper classes. In our present-day small apartments and houses with their restricted space, we mostly have to manage without such an ideal "home" for our tropical fern species.

Glossary of terms

Bark compost
Ready-made compost containing bark humus as the main component. A certain nutrient content and pH values of 5.5-7 should be provided by this type of compost. There are many different types and ferns should be given a nutrient-poor grade.

Bark humus
Chopped, shredded bark, mainly from conifers, which is used in proportions of 30-60 percent as a component of compost. Coarse bark humus improves the ventilation of compost and is, therefore, particularly suitable for epiphytic ferns.

Bulbils
Small immature bulbs or buds that form on shoots or on leaves (see p. 25). Small offset plantlets may form from these.

Epiphyte
A way of living that involves plants (epiphytes) growing on trees without using them for food so they are not parasitic (see p. 5).

Fertile
Fruitful; in the case of ferns this means they form spores.

Frond
Part of a multi-feathered leaf.

Heterophyllia
The occurrence of two different types of leaves on one plant. In many ferns both fertile and sterile fronds are formed. The sterile fronds usually have shorter stalks and possess broader surfaces. The fertile ones have longer stalks, possess narrower pinnae, and stand stiffly upright which is advantageous for the distribution of spores.

Indusium
A thin layer of skin (see illustration 1b, p. 8) which covers and protects the developing sori of many ferns. The shape of the indusium is characteristic of individual genera and species. Where these have been replaced by leaf edges which curl backward, they are called pseudo-indusium (see illustration 2, p. 8).

Leaf rib
The central stem of a feathered leaf (see illustration 6a, p. 9).

Peat compost
Ready-made compost consisting of bog peat with an established nutrient content and a pH value of 5-6. Nutrient-poor peat compost is suitable for ferns.

pH factor
Degree of acidity. For most indoor ferns a medium acid pH compost of 5-6 will be favorable.

Prothallium
Part of the sexual generation of ferns. A flat, often heart-shaped prothallium (see illustration 1d, p. 8) develops from the fern spore.

Rhizome
Thickened shoots which develop horizontally, usually underground, as storage or reproduction organs. In some fern species, like *Davallia*, they also grow above ground (see p. 43).

Sorus (plural sori)
Groups of spores which form different shapes (see illustrations 2-5, pp. 8-9). They form on the under sides of fern fronds.

Sporangium (plural sporangia)
Capsules with stalks in which the spores develop and out of which they are catapulted when ripe (see illustration 1c, p. 8).

Spores
Single-cell propagation units which form on the under sides of the fern fronds.

Standard compost
Ready-made compost made up of 60-80 percent by volume of bog peat and 20-40 percent by volume of loam with a varying nutrient content. The standard types possess a pH factor of 5.5-6.5 The types containing a low-dosage controlled-release fertilizer are suitable for ferns.

Sterile parts
Non-fertile parts which do not produce spores.

Terrestrial
Growing on the ground (see p. 5).

Variegated
Multi-colored leaves; for example, green and white, green and yellow, and green and red.

Botany

Alternating generations

Although ferns belong to the group referred to as higher plants, they do not form flowers or seed. Their life cycle demonstrates a clear alternation of generations. As non-scientists we are most familiar with one part of this cycle, namely the mature fern plant.

The sporophyte: This is the correct name for the actual fern plant, i.e. the spore-forming generation. The minute spores develop on the under sides of the fronds in capsules (see illustrations 1a and 1b). They are formed through division which means they have only half a set of chromosomes (haploid). Ripe spores are catapulted out of the capsules (see illustration 1c) and

distributed by the wind. When they settle in ideal conditions, they begin to germinate and are now called gametophytes.

The prothallium (see illustration 1d) develops from a germinating gametophyte. It is small and flat, with lobes (usually heart-shaped), and, apart from one section below the heart-shaped notch, consists of only one layer of cells which also have only half a set of chromosomes. This structure is green, however, and able to photosynthesize just like the leaves of a mature plant. Root-like, hair-shaped growths (rhizoids) anchor the prothallium firmly in the ground. The sexual organs develop on the under side of the prothallium, thus representing the second stage of sexual generation. The female cells (archegonia) form in the multicellular region beneath the heart-

2 Spore clusters under the rolled back leaf edges of Adiantum.

shaped notch. Their lower section, containing the ova, is sunk into the tissue of the prothallium, the upper part rears up like a neck. The male cells (antheridia) form between the root-like growths (rhizoids). They will later release mobile sperm (spermatozoa) which swim toward the female cells and fertilize the ova. For all of this to take place, the prothallium must become wet through the action of rain or dewdrops. The fusion of a sperm and an ovum, each of which carries half a set of chromosomes, creates a single-celled zygote which now contains a full (diploid) set of chromosomes. The zygote begins to grow into a mass of cells called an embryo and a new fern plant develops directly from this (see illustration 1e). As soon as the plant is large enough to survive on its own, the prothallium withers and dies.

Spores, sporangia, sori

The shape of the spores and the sporangia (spore capsules) differs according to species. The sporangia are grouped together in characteristic clusters called sori (see illustration 1b). During their development, they are usually protected by growths on the leaves (veils, indusia), by hairs or by scales. If they are shielded by

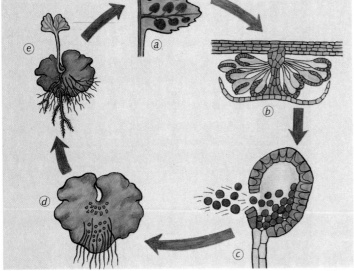

1 Alternating generations: (a) leaflet bearing clusters of spores (sori); (b) a cross section through a sorus with its spore capsules and veil; (c) ripe spores are catapulted out of the capsule; (d) a prothallus; (e) a new plant develops after fertilization.

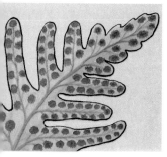

Circular spore capsules on *Polypodium*.

4 On Pteris, the spore clusters line the edges of the leaf fronds.

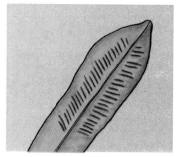

5 Lines of sori on Asplenium.

rolled-up leaf edges, they are referred to as pseudo-indusia (false veils). These occur in maidenhair fern (*Adiantum*) (see illustration 2) or in *Pteris* (see illustration 4).

The sori may be completely circular, as in *Polypodium* (see illustration 3). Among *Polystichum*, they bear shield-shaped veils. *Nephrolepis* possess kidney-shaped sori. *Davallia* form urn-shaped indusia. Interesting patterns are created by long lines of sori. In *Blechnum* they run along the narrow feathers very close to the central ribs; in *Pteris* or *Pellaea* along the edges of the leaves. In the case of *Asplenium* species (see illustration 5), which are sometimes called necklace ferns, they are arranged in stripes set diagonally toward the central rib. In *Platycerium* the sporangia, which take the form of brown or black markings, cover entire areas of the under sides of the leaves (see page 51). Depending on the species, these can be found on the tips of leaf lobes or beneath inward-curving leaves.

What is a frond?

Fronds are the very finely divided leaves of ferns, which consist of many small feathery sections which grow from one central leaf stem, rib or rhachis (see illustration 6a).

Single-feathered (pinnate) fronds are single, undivided feathery leaves (see illustration 6b) growing from the main leaf rib; for example, *Nephrolepis*.

In double-, triple-, or multi-feathered fronds (bipinnate), the feathers are divided two or more times (see illustration 6c). Examples include *Polystichum tsus-simense* (double), *Davallia trichomanoides* (three to four divisions).

Divided fronds: Here the division of the leaf does not reach quite as far as the central leaf rib. Example: *Phlebodium aureum*.

Other shapes of leaves: Ferns also occur with hand-shaped, divided fronds (*Doryopteris pedata*) or with coarsely lobed leaves (*Platycerium*). Undivided leaves frequently occur among *Asplenium* or *Polypodium*. For an overview of the many different shapes of leaves, see pages 10 and 11.

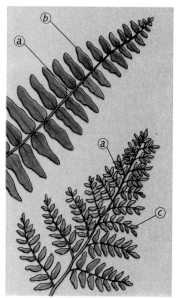

6 The structure of a leaf:
(a) leaf rib;
(b) simple leaflets;
(c) multi-feathered fronds.

Leaf shapes

Ferns surprise us with their great variety of shapes of fronds. Alongside simple structures, like undivided leaves (3, 8) or single-feathered ones (2, 5, 7), there are also more complex, divided ones (1).

In individual varieties you can often find feathers with curly ends. Sometimes, different gradations of feather may occur on the very same plant. In the lower sections of a frond the lateral feathering may be larger and more divided, while toward the tip there is more simple feathering. One can also often observe a mixture of divided structures (6). Variations also occur in the production of large single feathers (4) and in the varying structure of the leaf edge which may be dentate (2), wavy (5), or lobed (8).

1 *Adiantum raddianum*
   "Fragrantissimum".
2 *Cyrtomium falcatum.*
3 *Hemionitis arifolia.*
4 *Pteris cretica "Albolineata."*
5 *Nephrolepis exaltata "Teddy
   Junior."*
6 *Pteris fauriei.*
7 *Blechnum gibbum.*
8 *Asplenium nidus "Fimbriatum."*

A warm, moist, shady position

Asplenium nidus.

With their fresh green color and luxuriant growth, healthy ferns bring a hint of the tropical rain forest to your home or office. Naturally, it is a good idea to gather information on the kind of conditions these plants require before buying one so that your efforts will be crowned with success.

The ideal position for indoor ferns

Ferns of one species or another are at home in all the many different climatic regions of our planet.
Not all ferns, however, are happy to be grown indoors. Those that can be cultivated successfully inside our houses originate mainly from tropical or subtropical climates. Very often they come from rain forests where they grow on river banks, around springs, on mossy rocks, or as epiphytes on tree trunks. Gardeners try to replicate these conditions for such plants in warm, shady greenhouses with high humidity. Indeed, indoor ferns feel right at home in the tropical houses of botanical gardens. Moving into a modern house or apartment, however, often requires drastic adaptation from such plants. To ensure that they are able to flourish in a regular room, certain minimum requirements with respect to temperature, humidity, and light must be fulfilled.

Temperature

Ferns with tropical origins, like many maidenhair (*Adiantum*), *Davallia* and *Platycerium* species, depend on even temperatures all year round. The ideal temperature in many cases is 77° F (25° C) but the usual room temperatures of 64-68° F (18-20° C) will be sufficient. During the winter or at night, the temperature may even sink to 61° F (16° C).
Ferns from subtropical or temperate regions, on the other hand, require slightly lower temperatures. Among these are *Adiantum hispidulum, Cyrtomium falcatum, Pellaea rotundifolia* and *Polystichum tsussimense.* As a rule, they can manage at 61° F (16° C) in winter and even at 54° F (12° C) at night.

Humidity

A basic problem is that the air in our centrally heated living rooms is far too dry for ferns. High humidity is particularly important for maidenhair fern (*Adiantum*), *Blechnum* and *Nephrolepis.* These ferns will thrive best in either an enclosed plant picture window or in a glass case. An alternative is to stand these plants in rooms where the humidity rises, at least temporarily, to above the average, for example in a bathroom or kitchen. In other rooms additional measures to raise the humidity will have to be sought (see p. 18).

Light

Ferns are reckoned to be undemanding with respect to light requirements. A couple of species do grow on the edges of woods or on cliffs where they are exposed to sun and wind, but none of the indoor ferns can cope with direct sunlight. This does not mean, however, that all species want to be in darkness. For most, a little filtered sunlight is ideal – a situation referred to as semi-shady.
East- and west-facing windows which receive only morning or evening sunlight are, therefore, ideal positions.
North-facing windows are only suitable for ferns that like dark positions (see table, p. 14).
South-facing windows are normally not suitable for ferns. If you do not want to do without ferns in such a position, make sure that in the spring and summer there is some shade during the middle of the day or move the plants away from the window.

Ferns in an aquarium
This arrangement is not only an attractive feature, it also ensures excellent conditions for the plants due to its increased humidity.

My tip: Do not use your own perception of brightness as a measure for the light requirements of the plants. A position far to the back of a room, behind thick drapes, against an outside wall, or in a corner may be too dark even for a fern. An accurate reading of the particular light intensity of any spot can be obtained from a luxmeter (obtainable from garden centers). Indoor ferns require at least 500-1,000 lux, depending on species.

Buying ferns

Fern plants can be found in nurseries, florists, and garden centers. Accurate information on care, etc. is generally only available in specialty outlets.

Beware of plants:
● with meager growth
● with deformed leaves
● with brown leaves, feathers or leaf tips (exception: the sterile leaf funnels of *Platycerium*)
● with dried up rootstocks
● with webs or pests on them.

Introducing plants to a new environment
● While the plant is settling down, ensure that the best conditions are maintained, particularly sufficient humidity. The plants will have been accustomed to ideal conditions in a greenhouse and will require a certain amount of time to adapt to new circumstances, after which they are often surprisingly resistant.
● Newly purchased plants should not be transplanted immediately into larger pots. Usually, purchased ferns should not need to be repotted for a year or more.
● Do not start fertilizing for about four weeks as the compost in the pot nearly always contains enough fertilizer (see p. 17).

The right fern for the right position in your home

Ferns for shady positions
Asplenium species
(see pp. 38-39)
Cyrtomium (see p. 42)
Davallia (see p. 43)
Didymochlaena (see p. 44)
Microlepia (see p. 45)
green-leafed *Pteris* species
(see pp. 54-55)

Ferns that can cope with low humidity
Asplenium nidus (see pp. 38-39)
Cyrtomium (see p. 42)
Pellaea (see p. 48)
Phlebodium (see p. 49)
Platycerium
(see pp. 50-51)
Polystichum tsus-simense
(see p. 53)

Ferns that are suitable for hydroculture
Adiantum
(see pp. 36-37)
Asplenium nidus
(see pp. 38-39)
Cyrtomium
(see p. 42)
Nephrolepis
(see pp. 46-47)
Pellaea
(see p. 48)
Phlebodium
(see p. 49)
Polypodium
(see p. 52)
Pteris
(see pp. 54-55)

Ferns for hanging containers
Adiantum
(see pp. 36-37)
Asplenium species
(see pp. 38-39)
Davallia (see p. 43)
Nephrolepis (see pp. 46-47)
Platycerium (see pp. 50-51)

Ferns to grow as epiphytes
Asplenium antiguum
(see pp. 38-39)
Davallia (see p. 43)
Nephrolepis (see pp. 46-47)
Platycerium (see pp. 50-51)

Ferns for moss pillars
Asplenium antiguum
(see pp. 38-39)
Davallia (see p. 43)
Nephrolepis (see pp. 46-47)
Platycerium (see pp. 50-51)

Small ferns for bottle gardens
Actiniopteris australis
(see p. 56)
Adiantum "Fritz Luthi" (see pp. 36-37)
Doryopteris (see p. 44)
Hemionitis arifolia
(see p. 57)
Pellaea (see p. 48)
Polystichum tsus-simense
(see p. 53)
small *Pteris* species
(see pp. 54-55)

Creating a tropical rain forest

Many people think ferns are "difficult" indoor plants. Providing you consider their special requirements, however, you will be surprised how well they flourish inside your home. If you are able to reproduce similar conditions to those found in a tropical rain forest, these plants will be almost no bother to look after.

sting ferns.

hen grown in ideal conditions (see 12), indoor ferns create no more ork than most other plants, requir-ʒ only watering, fertilizing, the ːcasional misting, and repotting. ✓ comparison with flowering ants, there is less work as no ːad flowers need to be removed. ɔr will you need to vary the day, ʒht, or seasonal temperatures as ˥ns like regularity and even tem-ɹratures all the time. You will have ˥en less work if you are able to ffer your ferns a greenhouse, an ːclosed plant window, or even a ɔsed glass case which all contain ːeir own climates. Usually, how-er, such facilities are not available ˥ successful care will require a .le time and effort.

atering
ɹr main drinking water contains rious substances, some of which ˥ction as nutrients for plants and ˥ers which can have quite a ˥rmful effect on them, particularly if they are present in large quantities. The quality of your main water will depend mainly on its hardness, the total mineral salts content, and any specifically harmful substances.

Water hardness: If possible, do not use hard water for watering your ferns. There are two different types of hardness to consider.
● One measure is defined by the amount of calcium and magnesium salts. Water with a figure of more than 15 degrees Clark is considered to be medium hard.
● Carbonate hardness of the water is a determining factor for plants as it causes the pH value to rise in the compost when you water. When this happens, certain nutrients (trace elements in particular) can no longer be absorbed properly by the plant.

How to obtain soft water
● Collect rainwater.
● Put softening agents in the water. These can be obtained in powder or liquid form.

● Watering cans with special filter fixtures are very practical.

NB: Water that is too soft or water derived from certain water-softening installations can lead to just as many problems as water that is too hard. In addition to lacking impor-tant calcium and magnesium ions, the high content of potassium ions that is obtained through the soften-ing process will have a damaging effect on the plants.
My tip: The best thing to do is to mix softened water (or rainwater) with main water or to water alter-nately with one and then the other. The harder the main water is, the larger the amount of softened water you will need.

Total mineral salt content: Ferns belong among the species of plants that are particularly sensitive to salts. For this reason, the total min-eral salt content should not be too high.
Substances with a negative effect are mainly sodium and chloride. In concentrations that are too high they will impair the growth and health of the plants.

My tip: You will be able to find out about the relative values of your own main water from your local water utility. The following values should not be exceeded on a long-term basis:
● hardness: 13 degrees Clark
● sodium: 50 mg/4 cups (1 liter)
● chloride: 50 mg/4 cups (1 liter).

Ferns feel particularly comfortable in the high humidity of a bathroom.

Watering with care

Ferns are known to love humidity and will react extremely sensitively to a dry rootstock.

Avoid drying out: If, for example, you forget to water maidenhair fern (*Adiantum*) for several days in a row, the rootstock will dry out and the splendor of fresh green fronds will turn into withered, pale green or brown rags that will not recover even after extensive watering. The worst thing about this process is that the plant does not "warn" you over a period of time with slowly wilting leaves, but withers suddenly. If the tips of the young fronds are hanging down limply, it may already be too late for the entire plant.

No waterlogging: This will be caused by watering the plant too often or too much and then leaving the excess water in the bottom of the dish or potholder. It has a particularly devastating effect on ferns. Waterlogged roots can no longer obtain enough oxygen from the compost, which they need in order to absorb water and nutrients.

Follow the golden rule:
Watering indoor ferns the right way means keeping them evenly moist. If you water by hand, you should check the moisture in the compost daily with a fingertip and, when it is needed, give the ferns enough water to make the rootstock quite moist. After about fifteen minutes, tip away any excess water lying in the dish underneath.

ecial watering methods for
door ferns

semi-automatic watering sys-
m using clay pegs (see p. 18) is
rticularly well suited to ferns as
s method ensures constant, even
isture in the rootstock. One clay
g is inserted in every pot and the
gs are connected to a storage
ntainer, holding water or fertilizer
lution, by means of a thin hose.
e plant sucks up water from the
mpost and this water is constant-
replenished from the storage con-
ner through the porous clay pegs.
e moisture in the compost can be
gulated by setting the storage
ntainer at different levels in
spect to the plant pot. If it is on
e same level as the plant, more
isture will penetrate the compost
an when it is on a lower level.
en if you do switch over to this
ethod of watering you should still
eck the moisture in the rootstock
gularly to begin with and, if nec-
sary, place the storage container
gher or lower. After a while all
ur efforts will be well rewarded
d, later on, you will only need to
eck occasionally and top up the
orage container every so often. In
dition, over a period of time you
ll gradually learn how much water
ur plants consume and will be
le to estimate how many days at
time you can leave your plants on
eir own if you want to go away.
mersing is another ideal method
r watering ferns. This method is
rticularly favorable for plants in
cker baskets or for plants grow-
g on small epiphyte trunks. It is
so perfectly well suited to ferns
owing in pots as, by this method,
e rootstock is able to absorb
enty of water.
ethod: Immerse the entire plant,
its pot, in a bucket of water long
ough for air bubbles to stop ris-
g. Then let the excess water run
vay into a washbasin or bathtub

for about fifteen minutes. If you
happen to have forgotten to water,
immersing the plant in water is a
good first-aid measure. Afterward
cut off any dried up fronds. If the
plant was not left dry for too long, it
should produce new shoots.

Fertilizing

Plants in pots have only a limited
amount of space for their roots to
grow, along with relatively little
compost at their disposal, so nutrients are used up relatively quickly.
The possibility for plant nutrients to
be supplied from deeper layers of
soil or through the production of
humus, as would be the case in the
wild, is not an option for pot plants.
For this reason, you must make
sure there is an adequate
substitute.
*Suitable fertilizers for indoor
ferns:* The nutrients required by
ferns can be divided up by quantity
into main nutrients and trace elements. The main nutrients include
nitrogen (N), phosphorus (P), potassium or potash (K), magnesium
(Mg), calcium (Ca), and sulphur (S).
Use a liquid multi-nutrient compound fertilizer for your indoor
ferns, in which phosphorus and
potassium occur in a balanced
ratio. This information should be
listed on the packaging in the form
N + P + K ; for example, in the ratio
8 + 8 + 6. Ordinary liquid fertilizers,
available from garden centers, are
also suitable. They usually contain
the necessary trace elements of
iron, manganese, copper, zinc,
molybdenum, and boron.
A simple and time-saving way of
supplying nutrients is by the use of
controlled-release fertilizers. These
products release nutrients gradually
into the compost and, over many
weeks, ensure an even replenish-
ment without the mineral salt concentration rising too much.
How to fertilize correctly: Keep the

dose for ferns very low. In the case
of liquid fertilizers, half the amount
recommended for green plants will
be sufficient. The concentration to
use is normally 0.05% which is the
equivalent of about 1 teaspoon (0.5
g) fertilizer per 4 cups (1 liter) of
water. You may give liquid fertilizer
in water when watering, add it to
water used for immersing, or even
occasionally spray it onto the
plants.
For most ferns it is best to give a
dose of fertilizer at intervals of two
weeks. Some require more nutrients
and therefore need a weekly dose
of fertilizer; others manage on a
dose every four weeks. Exact
instructions as to quantities of fertilizer for different genera are given in
the plant descriptions on pages
34-59.
In their natural environment tropical
ferns are not used to a clearly
defined change of seasons nor to
the alternation of growing and dor-
mant periods during the year. In a
temperate climatic region, however,
they are practically forced to endure
a rest period in the winter due to
the decreased amount of light. For
this reason, you should fertilize only
in the spring and summer as, during
the rest of the time, their nutrient
requirement is not very high under
ordinary indoor conditions.

Raising the humidity and providing water
(a) Stand the pot on an upside-down saucer in a dish of water.
(b) Stand the pot in a larger pot lined with peat.
(c) Watering with clay pegs.

Humidity

Most ferns demand high humidity and will, therefore, be particularly comfortable in a greenhouse, an enclosed plant picture window, a glass case, or a bottle garden. A warmish conservatory containing lots of other plants will also engender enough humidity for ferns.

Things are a little more difficult in a room also lived in by humans. Dry air rising from a radiator on to a windowsill is like poison for most species of fern. The following suggestions will help to increase humidity.

● Do not stand the plants on their own but in groups. This will improve the mini-climate.

● Frequent misting of the plants. This is a lot of work, however. Also, some species, such as *Blechnum* and *Platycerium*, do not like water lying on their leaves.

● Ensure indirect humidity by means of water evaporators on your radiators or with electric humidifiers. It is also helpful to stand the fern on top of an upside-down saucer in a dish filled with water (see illustration a, above). An alternative is to place the fern pot inside another pot lined with moist peat (see illustration b, above).

Repotting

With some fern species, any space available in a pot is usually quickly filled up with vigorous root formation. Such species ought to be repotted once a year. However, many indoor ferns do not form a very vigorous root system and should only be repotted when necessary. All pot plants should receive fresh compost from time to time as salts tend to accumulate through watering and fertilizing or the compost may become acidic through waterlogging.

When to repot: The best time for this is in the spring as the plants can then start their new growth phase under ideal circumstances and will also recover from planting stress more easily.

What container to use: You may use clay or plastic pots for ferns. The plants will not dry out so fast in plastic pots, although a clay pot will tend to smooth over any mistakes in care (too much watering, for example) as water can evaporate through the porous walls. The important thing is that the new pot is not too large; as a rule, one that has a diameter ¾ in (2 cm) larger than the last pot will be sufficient. In the case of epiphytic ferns, it is

often advisable to remove only the loose compost and to put the plants back into the same sized pots.

The right compost: Compost give the plants a secure footing and should supply water, nutrients, an air. It is important, therefore, to us air- and water-permeable compos Ready-made composts containing low supply of nutrients or controlle release fertilizer are ideal for indoo ferns. These are standard compos composed of peat and loam, peat compost, or bark compost.

Because of its good drainage and ventilation properties, coarse bark compost is recommended for use with epiphytic ferns but you could also use orchid compost for these

My tip: Quality composts give an indication of their nutrient content and pH values on the packaging. Seek the advice of an exerienced member of staff at a good plant nursery or garden center when buy ing compost for your ferns. Do not simply buy compost for "indoor plants" nor the cheapest compost for sale.

How to repot

● Hold the pot in one hand and th bottom of the plant in the other an turn the whole thing upside down.

Repotting: Choose a pot that is no too large. Set the fern on layers of compost and drainage material.

18

Briefly tap the rim of the pot on edge of a table or similar until rootstock is loosened from the

Remove loose compost.
In the case of large pots, place a inage layer of Hortag (clay pel-) on the bottom.
Put in compost, leaving room for rootstock.
Now use one hand to place the nt in the middle of the new pot I use the other hand to shovel in sh compost (see p. 18).
Leave a watering "gulley" and ss the compost down lightly.
Water the repotted fern well.

rns in hydroculture

ne fern species are only offered sale as hydroculture plants (see 14). With this method of cultiva-n, the plants are rooted in Hortag I are supplied with water and rients by means of a nutrient ution. Plants in this type of dium are easy to care for as they ed to be watered less often and u cannot make many mistakes :ause the water requirement can read on a gauge. Ferns in hydro-ture are treated the same way as er plants in this medium. The in thing is that you should only er use soft water and give half the ilizer dose recommended for er green plants.

Fronds of Microlepia unfurling.

Displaying your ferns

Wooden baskets
Wooden baskets are available from some florists but you can also weave them yourself out of untreated, narrow, spruce battens about ¾ in (2 cm) thick.

These containers are variants on hanging containers and are very suitable for epiphytic ferns and *Platycerium* in particular.

How to plant in wooden baskets
Line the container with thin, non-rotting fabric so that fine particles of compost cannot fall through the gaps. Use coarse compost, such as bark compost, or orchid compost. Bed the plant loosely in the compost.

Care: Plants in wooden baskets are never watered but obtain water and nutrients through immersing (see p. 17).

Add fertilizer to the water for immersing depending on the requirements of the individual plant.

Fern pillar
(illustrations 1 and 2)
Almost all epiphytic plants are suitable for this arrangement because of their unusual and attractive eye-catching features. In addition, plants that normally grow as groundcover can be used to fill up the gaps between the ferns on the pillar, such as *Selaginella*, *Soleirolia soleirolii*, *Fittonia verschaeffetii*, or climbing ficus (*Ficus pumila*). For this structure you will need a very large, heavy dish or bowl that will provide a firm base for the pillar, a section of plastic pipe as the stable nucleus of the pillar, rust-free, fine-mesh wire, moss, compost, a cardboard tube, and a wooden stick.

Method
● Form the wire mesh into a cylinder. The thicker the cylinder, the greater its stability!

● Stand the cardboard roll inside the wire cylinder (only needed as a filling aid), and stand the plastic pipe in the center of the former (see illustration 1).

● From the bottom upward, place layers of moss between the cardboard roll and the wire mesh and press it down lightly by hand so that the outer surface of the moss can be seen through the wire mesh.

● Now insert the compost between the plastic pipe and the cardboard roll. Lightly press it in, using the stick, and make sure that no pockets of empty space remain.

● While inserting the compost, gradually draw the cardboard roll upward.

● If you want to place a plant right at the top of the pillar, make the plastic pipe a little shorter than the roll of wire mesh and the compost layers.

● Firmly anchor the pillar into the container used as a base with the help of Hortag or stones (see illustration 2). Additional ferns can be inserted in this medium too.

1 Stand a plastic pipe in a roll of cardboard inside a cylinder of wire mesh. Insert moss between the wire mesh and the cardboard. Insert compost between the plastic pipe and the cardboard roll. Cut open the wire and insert the ferns.

How to plant
● Cut open a few of the wire strands and push the wire and moss apart (see illustration 1).

● Insert the rootstock of the plan

● Carefully push the wire togethe again.

Care: Thoroughly mist the pillar o plants once daily. At intervals of t weeks add a liquid compound fer izer to the misting water (half the recommended dose!).

2 Bed the pillar firmly in the container with the help of stones. Other ferns in pots can be placed among the stones. Spray daily.

...iphyte trunk

...u will need a piece of tree trunk
... a large, gnarled branch with
...ks, moss, thin, rust-proof wire, a
...ge, heavy pot with a firm base,
...ment, and stones or Hortag. All
...the epiphytic ferns that can be
...ed for a pillar are also suitable for
...s arrangement. Species with
...ove-ground rhizomes which
...ep along the trunk, such as
...vallia and *Polypodium*, are partic-
...rly attractive. The lower parts of
... trunk, where conditions are
...ays a little moister, can also be
...ed for attaching terrestrial ferns
... *Doryopteris pedata* or *Pteris*.

...ethod

... Cement the branch or trunk into
...container.

... Cover the surface with stones,
...rtag or moss.

... Remove the ferns from their
...ts. In the case of very large root-
...ocks, remove a little of the
...mpost.

... Wrap moss around the roots and
...cure this with the wire.

... Using the wire, secure all plants
...epared in this way to the trunk or
...anch, preferably above a thick-
...ed knot or in a fork so that the
...re cannot slip downwards. Use
...tra moss to help to fix the plant.
...e thicker the layer of moss, the
...s the risk of the roots drying out.
...e plants should be firmly secured
...t without tying the roots and rhi-
...mes too tightly.

...**riation:** Individual plants can also
... tied to a small piece of wood or
...ction of cork and hung up.

...**s on care:** Plants on large epi-
...yte trunks will flourish best if the
...tire trunk is enclosed in a glass
...se or enclosed plant picture win-
...w. If you cannot provide such an
...angement, you will need to spray
... entire trunk at least once daily
...roughly or, better still, several
...es daily. Small specimens can be
...mersed in water baths. Fertilize in

the same way as for the fern pillar
(see p. 20).

A bottle garden

(illustrations 3a-3c)
Large-bellied glass containers of all
kinds are suitable. Use only the
smaller types of ferns, such as
*Pellaea rotundifolia, Polystichum
tsus-simense, Selaginella* or small
Pteris. A bottle garden is the ideal
environment for certain rare small
ferns that are difficult to grow in a
room because the humidity is too
low or they are too sensitive to drying out. Among these are
Actiniopteris australis and
Hemionitis arifolia.

Method

● Using a funnel made of cardboard, fill the bottom of the bottle
with fine pebbles or Hortag to act
as a drainage layer (see illustration
3a).

● Add enough compost on top of
this, making sure that the root of
the plant will still have sufficient
room.

● Use a spoon and a fork which

are tied to sticks as extended planting tools (see illustration 3b).

● Use these to insert the plants
carefully and lightly press down the
compost with the spoon (illustration
3c).

● Finally, water and close the bottle. If there is a lot of condensation,
open it for a while now and then.
Containers with small openings
need not be closed at all as the
moisture will remain in the open
glass for a long while and you may
not need to water again for several
weeks.

3 *Planting a bottle garden*
(a) *Use a funnel to insert first Hortag or another drainage layer, then compost.*
(b) *Use long-handled tools to insert the little plants.*
(c) *Press down with the spoon. Finally, water very gently and carefully.*

21

Ferns in an east-facing window

An east-facing window is not only an ideal place for ferns as many other plants also love the morning sun which provides enough light without burning them with rays that are too intense.

Flowering plants or plants with variegated foliage create splashes of color and accentuate the soothing shades of the green ferns. The following plants go well with indoor ferns.

Flowering plants:
Achimenes hybrids, begonias (*Begonia* "Eliator" hybrids), *Catharanthus roseus*, *Dipteracanthus* species, patience-plants (*Impatiens* New Guinea hybrids), African violets (*Saintpaulia ionantha* hybrids) and *Streptocarpus* hybrids.

Foliage plants:
Begonias (*Begonia* rex hybrids), *Caladium* hybrids, *Calathea* species, *Cordyline fruticosa*, *Ctenanthe* species, *Dieffenbachia* species and hybrids, *Dracaena* species, *Fittonia verschaeffeltii*, *Hypoestes phyllostachya*, *Maranta leuconeura*.

Adding color to ferns
African violets will bring the green of the ferns to life. Back row (from left to right): Arachniodes adiantiformis, Nephrolepis exaltata "Corditas," Asplenium nidus, Asplenium dimorphum.
Front row: club mosses (Selaginella).

Propagating ferns

A safe nursery for young ferns

Cyrtomium.

How do you propagate plants that do not produce flowers or seed? Ferns solve this problem for themselves by forming spores. When these germinate, a gametophyte is produced and from this a prothallium then grows to produce male and female cells called gametes. When the male and female cells mature, the male sperm fertilizes a female ovum and a new fern plant begins to grow.

Propagation from the distribution of spores

By spreading spores yourself you can reproduce the natural propagation process and then observe the unique events of fern multiplication. It is, however, a difficult undertaking and not always crowned with success. For this reason very few nurseries specialize in fern propagation. The determined amateur gardener should try out this technique initially with one of the species that does not present too many difficulties, for example Cyrtomium or Pteris.

Spores: Spores can rarely be bought in the retail trade like seed. You may be lucky enough to have a growing fern that bears spores; otherwise you will have to obtain a frond with spore capsules from a friend or acquaintance. Some ferns produce spores almost all year round, others only under optimum conditions.

With most species you will need a lot of experience to determine exactly when the spores are ripe.

Unripe spores are useless for sowing. On the other hand, completely ripe spores are catapulted out of their cases and, because of their miniscule size and low weight, will be broadcast far and wide by the slightest movement of air. Collecting the spores must, therefore, be done shortly before this happens.

My tip: Very often the spore capsules are white or light green in color in their unripe state and turn brown at the point of maturity. In certain other species the mature spores are colored gray, yellow, or orange.

Harvesting spores

● Cut off a fern frond when the spores are ripe and wrap it in paper.

● Hang it up in a dry place for at least three days. When the ripe spores are catapulted out, they will be caught in the paper.

● Next, carefully remove any rotten or deformed spores.

● It is best to plant them right

away. The ability of fern spores to germinate may endure for only a few hours or for decades, depending on the species. If you do not want to sow them immediately, you should store the spores in a cool, dry place to prolong their ability to germinate.

How to sow: Place nutrient-poor compost (for example, seeding compost) in pots or small dishes. The best plan is to use new containers or else carefully clean used ones beforehand. Pour boiling water over the compost and let the excess water run away. This treatment ensures that any undesirable spores of algae, fungi, and mosses are killed off. When the compost is just lukewarm, sow the spores sparsely and use a fine mister to spray them with cooled, boiled water. Do not cover them with compost.

Care: The sown spores will require warmth (68-77° F/20-25° C) without direct sunlight. On no account should they be left to dry out. Spores sown in plastic containers should be covered with a pane of glass or plastic wrap. After about four to six weeks, little prothalli should develop from the spores (see illustration 1d, p. 8). Fertilization, which occurs on the under sides of the prothalli, will only succeed if a film of moisture is present. The first new leaves of the young fern plants (see illustration 1e) will form from the fertilized ova (depending on the species) three to eighteen months after sowing. From now on, you should remove the cover occasionally to harden off the young plants.

As soon as they are large enough to touch each other, they should be pricked out separately. When they are 2-4 in (5-10 cm) tall, the young plants can be planted singly or in small groups in little pots.

emionitis arifolia with a new plantlet emerging from a bulbil.

issue culture

ears ago, only sterile ferns could
e propagated from rhizomes.
owadays, using tissue culture,
mall sections of tissue can be
sed to generate a large number of
hole, identical plants. Specially
stalled equipment in laboratories
required for this method of culti-
ation. This process ensures that
ant lovers have access to ferns of
e highest quality at reasonable
rices. Today many varieties of
ephrolepis, *Platycerium*, *Pellaea*,
d *Davallia* are grown in this way.

It is really not practical for amateurs
to propagate ferns by this method
as totally sterile conditions must be
available. Unless your hobby is
actually biology rather than gardening, it is probably best to leave this
sort of thing to the experts and simply buy the ferns you want to grow.

In *Asplenium dimorphum* new
plantlets develop all over the fronds
along the leaf ribs.

Propagating

Creating the best possible conditions

A certain amount of basic knowledge is applicable to all methods of fern propagation.

The best time: Ferns can be propagated all year round but the ideal time is in the spring as the young plants then benefit from the higher intensity of light and do not have to endure the atmosphere of dry, centrally-heated air.

Compost: Seeding compost is suitable.

Care

● Carefully water the young seedlings and keep them evenly moist (not wet).

● Stand the pots in a warm position with air and compost temperatures of 68-77° F (20-25° C).

● The position should be bright but protected from direct sunlight.

● To ensure high humidity, bend rust-proof wire into an arch and push the ends into the pot. Draw a transparent plastic bag over this and tie it up (see illustration 2). If there is a great deal of condensation, take the bag off for a few hours now and again.

● As soon as new fronds have formed, the little plant can be gradually hardened off. This is done by removing the plastic bag for periods of time and then entirely.

● This is the time when very low doses of fertilizer can be given.

Dividing ferns

(illustration 1)

Division is suitable for ferns that spread over the entire surface of the pot and which produce short shoots or stunted rhizomes with shoots, such as maidenhair fern (*Adiantum*), *Polystichum*, and *Nephrolepis*.

Method. Remove the plant you want to divide from its pot and cut through the rootstock with a sharp knife so that two or more individual parts with a vigorous vegetation point and sufficient roots are created. The vegetation point represents the heart of each plant, from which new fronds will grow. Without it the newly divided fern would not be viable. Dead roots and leaves should be removed and the separate pieces planted in individual pots.

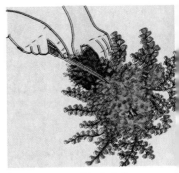

1 Dividing a maidenhair fern (Adiantum).

Rhizome cuttings

(illustration 2)

● In the case of rhizomes that grow above ground, for example those of *Davallia*, suitable places for dividing are easy to recognize.

● In the case of underground rhizomes, you will be able to recognize sections suitable for cutting off by the development of a group of new fronds on the compost surface.

Method

● Use a sharp knife to cut the rhizome into individual sections, each of which should have several bulbils. The bulbils are recognizable as the places from which fronds

2 A rhizome cutting with several buds is cut off and pegged to the compost.

3 Long runners can be pegged down on the surface of compost. Separate them as soon as new roots form.

emerge or as slight swellings. It is best if these rhizome parts have already produced roots as unrooted rhizome sections will not grow very well.

● The sections of rhizome that grew underground should be covered with compost to the same depth as before.

● The parts of rhizomes that grew above ground should be laid on the compost and pinned down with a rust-proof wire clamp.

● Further care: see page 26, column 1.

Propagating from shoots
(illustration 3)

Shoots from horizontal axils are developed mainly by *Nephrolepis*. When they come into contact with the soil, they grow roots and form new plants from their bulbils. This development can be encouraged by placing a pot of compost beside a *Nephrolepis* and then fixing shoots to its surface with clamps. After a while, the bulbils will produce new shoots. As soon as several fronds have developed, you can separate the young plants from the mother plant.

Further care: see page 26, column 1.

Offset plantlets
(Illustrations 4-6)

Vegetative propagation through offset plantlets occurs relatively widely in ferns. New, small plantlets form on the mother plant from the bulbils that grow in various places on the fronds. When they come into contact with the soil, they start producing roots.

In the case of *Adiantum caudatum*, they sit on the tips of the fronds that then hang down to touch the ground (see illustration 4).

In *Asplenium* species (see illustration 5 and p. 25), they form all over the frond in such large numbers that the fronds are forced downward and the plantlets thus make contact with the soil.

● In *Doryopteris pedata* and *Hemionitis arifolia* they develop at the base of the leaf stalk (see illustration 6 and p. 25).

Method: By bending the frond downward and pinning it to the compost with a wire, you will enable the offset to form roots while still attached to the mother plant. Make sure the humidity is high (see p. 26, column 1). When you can see roots, you can separate the plantlet from the parent and plant it in a pot.

Alternative: If you wish, you can cut off entire parts of fronds together with offset plantlets and lay them on compost. When the plantlets have taken root, they can be planted in individual pots.

Tubers
Of the few ferns that produce tubers, the best known is *Nephrolepis cordifolia*. The tubers develop on the underground rhizomes. If they are separated, together with part of the rhizome, and repotted, entire new plants will grow from them.

4 A breeder plantlet on the frond tip of *Adiantum caudatum*.

5 A breeder plantlet on the leaf rib of *Asplenium*.

6 A breeder plantlet at the point on the stem where the leaf emerges in *Doryopteris*.

First aid for your ferns

A delicate frond.

Compared to other groups of plants, ferns are rarely infested with pests. Far more often they are the victims of mistakes in care because their species-determined requirements have not been met. However, should unwelcome visitors appear, you will find some useful advice here.

Common mistakes in care

Withering fronds may signal a whole range of problems but are usually caused by too little or too much watering. Fading young fronds, as a rule, indicate lack of water. When you notice this, you should water immediately. The best thing to do in such cases is to immerse the whole plant in water (see p. 17).

On the other hand, if you give too much water, this will result in waterlogging and the entire plant will wither. If all the air spaces in the compost around the roots are filled with water, no oxygen will be available to the roots, which they need in order to absorb water and nutrients. In spite of a plentiful supply of water, the plant will die of thirst. A fern that is withering because of persistent waterlogging cannot be saved. The only thing left to try is to take the plant out of its potholder so that excess water can run away. Do not water again until the compost is slightly dry and then water sparingly in the future (see p. 16).

Dried up fronds are an indication that the rootstock of the fern has dried out. As long as this state of affairs is fairly recent, you can try to encourage the plant to produce new shoots by immersing the root-stock in water (see p. 17).

Pale green fronds: The adult fronds of some fern species do not actually wither but will lose their fresh green color and turn pale green. Finally, the feathery divisions of the frond fall off. These symptoms may indicate too much or too little water as well as a position that is too dark or too cool, particularly in the case of *Nephrolepis.* Check the rootstock with your finger to make sure the moisture content is correct and choose a position with enough warmth and light but out of direct sunlight.

Veins that turn brown and show up like lots of little lines on the feathery leaves of maidenhair fern (*Adiantum*) point to a position that is too cool and has high humidity. Place the maidenhair fern in a warmer position.

Brown edges to leaves are usually the result of humidity that is too low. In the case of *Asplenium* (see p. 30) they may also be the result of a position that is too cool. Raise the humidity level (see p. 18) and move the plant to a position that is sufficiently warm.

Dark brown, decaying parts of the leaves occur in *Platycerium* and *Blechnum* if they are misted and do not then dry off in a short space of time. These species do better if they are not misted all over but are supplied with indirect humidity (see p. 18).

Fungi and bacteria

Harmful fungi do attack ferns, particularly those that propagate by means of spores. The most frequent problem is gray mold which covers the sown spores with what looks like grayish-white fur. This leads to decay of the prothalli and young plants. The best remedy is good hygiene, as described in the chapter on propagation (see p. 24). Fungi or bacteria rarely occur on adult plants indoors. They are encouraged, however, by placing plants too close together, if they are too wet or if they do not have adequate ventilation.

Depending on the fungus species, infestation manifests itself through different symptoms. Gray mold forms a thick, gray white film which causes individual parts of the plant to decay and finally leads to the death of the entire plant. Other fungi cause irregular, gray to reddish-brown patches or growths on the leaves. In the case of *Asplenium nidus* bacteria may cause small, glassy spots to appear on the upper parts of the fronds, which may then spread rapidly in unfavorable circumstances.

In all diseases caused by fungi and bacteria, the infested fronds should be removed, you should refrain from wetting the plant and should offer a different position and less humidity. Combating the problem with synthetic agents (fungicides) is not usually worth the effort.

Animal pests

Among the few pests that occur on ferns it is gnats (*Diptera, Sciaridae*), scale insects, and spider mites that are met with most frequently. Occasionally you may also discover aphids, thrips, snails, slugs, and leaf blotch eelworm.

If a plant is infested with harmful organisms, you can try various remedies.

Mechanical means are time consuming but very effective and entirely non-toxic. They can be used for aphids, *Diptera, Sciaridae* and slugs and snails.

● Scale insects can be scraped off with a knife.

● Aphids can be washed off with water.

● In the case of *Diptera* and *Sciaridae*, it is usually sufficient to catch the adult insects and prevent them from laying more eggs. This job is successfully carried out by using sticky yellow tags (available in garden centers) which can be hung up near the plants. The small gnats are attracted by the yellow color and then get caught on the sticky surface of the yellow tags. You should also make sure that no stagnant moisture is left to lie around.

● Slugs and snails can be gathered up and removed.

A large fern on a tall plant table makes an attractive feature.

Biological control, by means of useful insects, can be tried in the case of an infestation with aphids, spider mites, or thrips. Useful insects like ladybirds, lacewings, gall midges, and predatory mites will prey on pests. Others, like ichneumon flies, lay their eggs in the larvae of the pests and, on hatching, the ichneumon larvae consume their hosts.

Washes, teas, or fermented brews are plant-based, pest-regulating agents that can be prepared at home. They are employed against aphids and spider mites as well as against fungal infections. The addition of an agent like dishwashing liquid, which will break the surface tension of water, will help the brew to stick to plant surfaces.

Brown edges will appear along the leaves of Asplenium if the air is too dry or the temperature too cool.

Chemical plant protection agents:
Among the plant protection agents obtainable in garden centers are insecticides and acaricides for use against pests. If at all possible, it is far better to leave these agents alone. It is true that they are broken down in the compost after a certain amount of time, but new compounds are created during this process and the effects of these have not yet been established. In addition, if these agents are used several times, strains of pests may develop that are immune to the effects of the agents.

Handling plant protection agents

● Seek advice from experts in garden centers when buying chemical plant protection agents.
● Protect your environment by not using sprays containing CFC propellant gases.
● Always follow the directions and advice on dosage given on the packaging meticulously.
● Before preparing any spray, work out the amount you will require so that all of the liquid is used up.
● Only spray outside.
● Do not spray on windy days and avoid letting a spray cloud drift into a neighbor's garden.
● Wear gloves and do not breathe in the mist.
● When spraying, make sure you spray as evenly as possible and wet the under sides of leaves thoroughly.
● Carry out the recommended number of treatments at the intervals prescribed by the manufacturer in order to eliminate successive generations of pests.
● Store plant protection agents in their original packaging out of reach of children and domestic pets and make sure they are locked away.

Warning

The employment of chemical plant protection agents and mineral oils is particularly undesirable for ferns as these plants are very sensitive to many agents, particularly plants with young fronds. Always test any such spray treatment on a few leaves first. A preferable alternative is to use agents that do not harm useful insects. In the past plant protection agents containing pyrethrum, an extract from a species of chrysanthemum, or synthetic related substances (pyrethroids) were considered to be without risk for humans or nature. You should, however, be very careful with these agents as they have been suspected of creating allergies, having mutagenic properties, causing cancer and having other harmful effects. The direct penetration of pyrethrum into the bloodstream, for example through a cut, is considered to be particularly dangerous.

Pest control

The most important method of control, particularly if you intend to use mechanical and biological remedies is the early recognition of pests. When the entire plant is covered in scale insects, it will be very difficult to gather them all by hand without merely spreading some of the young insects. When spider mite colonies have become established over the entire plant and have formed dense webs, predatory mites will never gain the upper hand.

With ferns that are cheap to buy
and commonly available on the
market, you should probably consider whether it is worth your while
using plant protection agents or
large amounts of your own time and
energy in combating pests rather
than simply discarding that particular plant and replacing it with a
healthy one. However, when you
have decided to attempt the rescue
of a much-loved specimen or a pre-
vious older plant, you should carry
out the treatment rigorously in order
to prevent renewed infestation.

The appearance, symptoms, and
control of the five most frequently
occurring pests in ferns are summa-
rized in the table on the right. In
addition to these pests, leaf blotch
eelworm may occasionally occur
and, in small greenhouses, conser-
vatories, or glass cases, you may
come across the occasional slugs
and snails.

Leaf blotch eelworm: You will
recognize an infestation by the dark
brown to black patches on leaves
that are clearly delimited by the leaf
veins. Cut off infested fronds and if
the symptoms persist, destroy the
entire plant.

Slugs and snails: Usually, they only
eat the leaves at night. In *Pteris*
they scrape off the under sides of
the leaves and let the upper side
remain as a transparent layer. Slugs
and snails that eat ferns do not
leave behind any telltale slime trails
so proof of their presence is not
always obvious. Collect the snails
early in the morning or stand small
dishes filled with beer around your
plants.

The most common pests on indoor ferns

Aphids mainly infest young shoots and rob them of nutrients by sucking the sap from them. This results in poor growth and crippled leaves. The honeydew excreted by the aphids may lead to an infestation with sooty mold fungus. Remedy: Rinse the aphids off with water; employ useful predatory insects or biological or chemical agents.

Gnats (Diptera, Sciaridae)
These are small, black gnats that run across the surface of the compost and fly up when you water. The larvae live in the compost and eat the roots. Infestation is encouraged by waterlogging. Remedy: Catch the gnats by hand or with the help of yellow tags; avoid waterlogging; ensure adequate ventilation.

Thrips: Symptoms are silvery, shiny patches and black excrement on the leaves. The insects are rarely visible as they live on the under sides of leaves and in other sheltered places and are very quick. They damage the plants by sucking the sap. Remedy: Use useful predatory insects or chemical plant protection agents.

Scale insects: Symptoms are brown-scaled insects on leaves, stalks, and rhizomes. They rob the plant of nutrients and cause disturbances in growth. Colonies of sooty mould fungus appear on the excreted honeydew. Remedy: Scratch off the insects; treat with synthetic insecticides or with tar oil.

Spider mites: Minute spider-like creatures, mostly on the under sides of leaves. Yellow patches will appear on the leaves. Dense webs with heavy infestation are encouraged by too low humidity and too warm a position. Remedy: Employ useful insects; spray with biological plant protection agents or synthetic acaricides.

Ferns and orchids

Ferns in many shades of green make the perfect foil for the splendor of orchid flowers. Most often it is the tropical species of these flowering and green plants that are grown indoors and they therefore usually have similar requirements as to care and the position they prefer. High humidity and good quality water are indispensable for both orchids and ferns.

When choosing orchids, consider their special needs with respect to temperature and light. Many orchids originate from mountainous regions in tropical countries where they are subjected to a wide range of changing temperatures both night and day. Certain species also require relatively high intensity of light. These special needs, which often may not correspond to the ideal conditions for tropical ferns, will have to be met when growing such plants on a windowsill if you want them to flower again and again.

In garden centers it is mostly orchid hybrids that are for sale; in other words, plants that have been created through crossing. Such orchids are both less demanding in respect of the above requirements and also often display vigorous growth and frequent flowering. They make ideal companion plants for indoor ferns.

The most beautiful indoor ferns

Clusters of spores.

With a huge selection of about 9,500 fern species to choose from, the fern-lover's passion for collecting need know scarcely any boundaries. Most of the ferns that can be cultivated indoors originate from tropical and subtropical climatic zones. There follows a selection of the most attractive genera, species and varieties usually obtainable from garden centers or nurseries.

Botanical nomenclature

The following descriptions include the botanical name of the plant followed by the common name (where appropriate).

The botanical name consists of the genus name, for example *Nephrolepis* (Greek: nephros = kidney, lepis = scale). This is always printed in italic script with a capital letter. It is followed by the species name, for example *exaltata* (Latin: exaltatus = growing tall), also in italics and always with a lowercase letter. These names have been adopted all over the world and help to avoid confusion.

They are also very useful for plant lovers as many species bear different common names in different parts of the world. For example, you can buy *Nephrolepis* under the name of sword fern. If the plant did not have a universally agreed Latin name, anyone trying to buy this plant from a florist might end up with a plant from a completely different genus, *Polystichum munitum*, also known as sword fern, which is used as greenery in flower arrangements.

Many plant names carry a third element, the variety name. This is always written with a capital letter and placed in inverted commas, for example *Nephrolepis exaltata* "Teddy Junior." This makes it clear that you are dealing with a variety of this plant species that was specially raised or created in cultivation.

A key to the listing of ferns

The fern genera described here are listed in alphabetical order according to their botanical names.
The individual descriptions begin with the most important species. The details refer to their size, appearance, shape of growth, and use of the plants as well as to the shape and color of the leaves, rhizomes, and spore clusters. References to related species and to the number of known species in a genus round off the information given. Following this is a short listing using the following keywords.

Family: Plant genera with the same features are grouped together in families by botanists. Membership of a family manifests itself above a through the ways in which the spore clusters are grouped.

Origin: This section tells us where each fern originates. The prevailing climate in these regions will offer valuable information as to the kind of position and care each fern will need. Even the prevailing mini-climate is of some importance and so relevant typical natural positions are described as is the type of growth (epiphytic or terrestrial).

Position: This keyword defines the requirements of the plant with respect to light, temperature, and humidity.

Care: This section gives exact details as to watering, fertilizing, and repotting.

Propagation: This section covers possible types of propagation (see pp. 24-27) which should be successful for the individual genera.

Pests, diseases: Pests and diseases that afflict the individual genera are named here.

My tip: Personal experience and special recommendations of the author.

Warning: This gives notes on toxic or skin-irritating substances contained in the plants.

oxic substances

ever ever eat any part of
our indoor ferns as many
ants have toxic proper-
es. Also make sure that
o children or domestic
ets are able or allowed
 eat parts of the plants.
ertain species contain
xic substances. For
xample, some *Davallia*
pecies contain
yanogenic glycosides.
pore-forming ferns may
igger skin allergies, par-
cularly *Arachniodes adi-
ntiformis*, which is used
s greenery in arrange-
ents of cut flowers and
 occasionally also
ffered as a pot plant.
eople known to have
lergies should avoid this
ant.

*he under sides of golden
rn (Pityrogramma)
aves look as if they have
een dusted with gold.*

The dainty, elegant fronds of maidenhair ferns.

Adiantum
maidenhair fern

Maidenhair ferns are considered to be among the most elegant representatives of ferns with their fresh green, fine, feathery leaves and thin, shiny black-brown stalks. About 200 species are known, out of which mainly species from the tropical regions are grown as indoor plants. There is also a species (*Adiantum capillus-veneris*) which occurs in western and southern Europe and is distributed as far as the Alps.

The genus is rich in different forms. In addition to single- to multi-feathered species and varieties, there is also a species with undivided, kidney-shaped leaves (*Adiantum reniforme*).

The individual types differ widely in the size of their feathery leaves. The leaves of *Adiantum raddianum* "Microphyllum" are minute. They give the plant a delicate appearance. However, even large-leafed species, such as *Adiantum peruvianum* whose feathery leaves can grow up to 2 in (5 cm) long, have a delicate appearance as the leaves are very thin.

Fertile and sterile fronds look the same in all *Adiantum* species. Spores are formed, particularly in older plants, along the edges of the fronds. The spore clusters are concealed beneath the curled-over edges of the leaves until they are mature.

● *Adiantum raddianum* and *Adiantum tenerum* are the two best known species. There are many varieties which possess double- or multi-feathered fronds. When they shoot, the young leaves are light green, or sometimes reddish, as, for example, in *Adiantum tenerum* "Scutum Roseum." In fully grown plants the fronds often droop slightly. They can be used as greenery in dainty bouquets of flowers.

Over 60 varieties of *Adiantum raddianum* have been registered, such as "Brilliantelse," "Goldelse," "Gracillimum," and "Fragantissimum." Varieties with variegated leaves are also available. The stalks of the variety "Fritz Lüthi" stand stiffly upright and form compact plants that are considered to be very long-lasting.

● *Adiantum fulvum*, a single-feathered species, whose leaves grow closely together around the leaf stem, appears very dense.

● *Adiantum hispidulum* has an atypical foot-shaped leaf division unlike other maidenhair ferns.

● *Adiantum caudatum* is an attractive hanging species with slender, single-feathered fronds that look very good in hanging containers.

Family: *Adiantaceae*, maidenhair ferns.

Origin: Central and South America, Africa and Asia, Polynesia, Australia, New Zealand, Madeira, Canary Islands. Mostly tropical and subtropical but also found in temperate regions.

The home of the tropical species is the rain forest. They occur as terrestrial ferns, often along the banks of streams, around springs, waterfalls, and in rock clefts.

Position: Bright but not sunny. Warm all year round (minimum 64° F/18° C). You must ensure the ferns have "warm feet." When they

36

The spore clusters of Adiantum raddianum.

The spore clusters of Adiantum peruvianum.

Adiantum hispidulum is a robust maidenhair fern.

ave been properly hard-
ned off, they will cope
ith night-time tempera-
res as low as 59° F
5° C). *Adiantum hispidu-
m, Adiantum fulvum*,
nd *Adiantum reniforme*
e suitable for cooler
aces. Nearly all species
nd varieties require high
umidity and will flourish
a glass case, an
nclosed plant picture
indow, or in a bottle
arden. Dry, centrally
eated air and drafts
hould be avoided.
are: Keep evenly moist
nd use soft water. Do
ot let it dry out or the
onds will wither very
pidly. If the plant has
ied out for only a short
me, immersing the root-

stock in water is helpful
(see p. 17). Also cut off
any brown fronds. The
plant should then begin to
shoot again. Give a little
less water in winter
(except in very warm
rooms). Give low doses of
fertilizer from the first
month of spring to the
first month of fall every
two weeks. Make sure
humidity levels are high
(see p. 18) and occasion-
ally mist over lightly.
Repot every year or two in
the spring. Ferns require
compost that absorbs
sufficient amounts of
water and still has good
drainage.
Propagation: From
spores or by dividing
larger plants. *Adiantum*

caudatum can be propa-
gated from offset plantlets
that form on the tips of
the fronds.
Pests, diseases: Aphids
on young shoots. Gray
mold in conditions that
are too wet. These plants
react very sensitively to
plant protection agents.
My tip: The bathroom is
an ideal position for maidenhair ferns as they feel
right at home in high
humidity.
Adiantum hispidulum is
considered to be a less
demanding species with
respect to humidity and
temperatures.

Asplenium nidus is the best known bird's nest fern.

Lines of spores on bird's nest fern.

Asplenium
bird's nest fern

Approximately 600 species of this genus are distributed all over the world. In addition to species from tropical and subtropical regions that are suitable as indoor plants, representatives of this species also occur in regions with a temperate climate. They often grow in particularly exposed spots, such as on rocks or walls and are widely distributed even in alpine regions. In northern Europe the following occur naturally: *Asplenium adiantum-nigrum*, *Asplenium rutamuraria*, *Asplenium septentrionale*,

maidenhair spleenwort (*Asplenium trichomanes*), and *Asplenium viride*. The species in this genus demonstrate a surprisingly wide range of shapes and forms. Ferns showing two completely different shapes of growth are used as indoor plants: the bird's nest ferns and the bulbiferous ferns. The giant bird's nest ferns possess undivided, large leaves, while the bulbiferous ferns have multi-feathered leaves. Tiny offset plantlets form on the latter's finely feathered fronds (see p. 25). The spore capsules are generally arranged in longish groups along the lateral veins in this genus.

● *Asplenium nidus*, the best-known bird's nest fern, forms large funnel-shaped rosettes with its undivided, spear-shaped leaves in which it is able to collect water and nutrients. If you have ever seen a giant specimen in a botanical garden, some of which attain a diameter of 7-10 ft (2-3 m), you will be able to imagine how these funnels are able to catch falling leaves and other organic material which then serve the fern as a source of nutrients. For this reason the bird's nest fern is often compared to a bromeliad. The dark brown to black central veins stand out attractively against the shiny

light green of the leaves. The spores are formed in the upper third of mature fronds, along the lateral veins. Sometimes the variety "Fimbriatum" is offered for sale. This has clearly lobed leaves. It grows very slowly.
● *Asplenium antiguum* is a bird's nest fern that has only recently appeared on the market. It is a species with narrower leaves that taper toward the tip. The leaf edges of the variety "Osaka" are wavy.
● *Asplenium bulbiferum*, *Asplenium daucifolium*, and *Asplenium dimorphum* belong to the group of bulbiferous ferns. They possess two to multi-feathered fronds. Tiny fer

Asplenium nidus "Fimbriatum" grows very slowly.

Asplenium antiguum is a bird's nest fern with narrow leaves.

antlets are formed from bulbils in the upper sections of the leaves. The fronds become heavy and then lean down to the ground where the young antlets take root. Asplenium dimorphum is considered to be the most resilient species of the bulbiferous ferns given here.

Family: Aspleniaceae.
Origin: Asplenium nidus, an epiphyte, is at home in the tropical rain forests of Africa, Asia and Australia. Asplenium antiguum originates in Japan. Bulbiferous ferns are found growing terrestrially in Australia, New Zealand, on Norfolk Island, in northern India and on the Mascarene Islands.

Position: Bird's nest fern semi-shady to bright; bulbiferous ferns semi-shady to shady. Room temperature should be even all year round but may drop to 61° F (16° C) during the winter. Around 54-59° F (12-15° C) may be sufficient for bulbiferous ferns in winter. The plants prefer high humidity but Asplenium nidus will cope with drier air.

Care: Bulbiferous ferns should be kept fairly moist all year round. Bird's nest ferns require medium watering. The funnels should be sprayed often or you could mist the entire plant. Give weak doses of fertilizer fort-nightly between the first month of spring and the first month of fall. Repot in the spring if required. Do not use very large pots for bird's nest ferns and keep the compost loose.

Propagation: From spores and plantlets.

Pests, diseases: Scale insects; brown edges to leaves are caused by too low humidity or too cool a position for Asplenium nidus.

My tip: Bird's nest ferns are eminently suitable for epiphyte trunks and fern pillars.

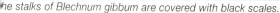
The stalks of Blechnum gibbum are covered with black scales.

A young frond.

Blechnum
hard fern

The European hard fern (Blechnum spicant) belongs in this genus. The majority of the 200 or so known species originate from the tropics and subtropics. Many form bright trunks with a rosette of single-feathered, lightly overhanging fronds at the top. These plants tend to remind one of palm trees. The leaves,

In a really favorable position Blechnum gibbum can attain an imposing size.

which have hardly any stalk, have strong central ribs. Usually the sterile fronds form broader feathery leaflets, the fertile ones only narrow leaves. The spore capsules form in long strips along the central ribs.

● *Blechnum brasiliense* develops into large specimens with stems up to 40 in (1 m) high. The young, reddish fronds unfurl from the center of the leaf rosette.

● *Blechnum gibbum* is generally offered for sale as a small pot plant but, given a favorable position, can also attain a considerable size.

Family: Blechnaceae.
Origin: Shady forests in

the tropics and subtropics of the southern hemisphere. They flourish as terrestrial ferns in moist to wet soils.

Position: Bright to semi-shady, no sunlight. Even room temperature all year round, not below 61° F (16° C) during the winter. Medium high humidity.

Care: Water plentifully in spring and summer but avoid waterlogging. Do not let it dry out or brown leaf tips will instantly appear. Several days of drought will kill the plant. Give weak doses of fertilizer every two weeks from the first month of spring to early fall. Do not spray the plant or mist it all as it is sensitive to wet leaves.

Ensure indirect humidity (see p. 18) and good ventilation. Younger specimens should be repotted once a year, older ones when necessary.

Propagation: From spores.

Pests, diseases: Aphids on young shoots; scale insects. Stagnant water on the fronds leads to glassy leaves, followed by black patches.

Cyrtomium falcatum "Rochfordianum" is attractive and extremely robust.

Cyrtomium
holly fern

The name of holly fern describes the appearance of this robust fern very well. While the young leaves are light green, the mature leaves are a shiny dark green and irregularly coarsely dentate, rather like the leaves of the European holly tree (*Ilex*). They look leathery, are simply feathered and have green, strong stalks that are covered, particularly in the lower sections, with dense brown scales. Circular clusters of spores are distributed all over the feathers. They turn from creamy white to brown as they ripen.

● Out of the ten known species, *Cyrtomium falcatum* is the one most frequently found as an indoor plant. The variety "Rochfordianum" is also widely available. It has deeply dentate, slit, feathery leaves.

● *Cyrtomium fortunei* is very similar to *Cyrtomium falcatum* but not often available from nurseries.

Family: *Aspidiaceae*.
Origin: Terrestrial fern from the temperate to subtropical regions of eastern Asia, Polynesia, Sri Lanka and South Africa.
Position: Semi-shady to bright, no direct sunlight. The plant loves cool, airy places. During the winter

the room temperature should not rise above 59° F (15° C). A brief drop to 36° F (2° C) will not harm it, provided it has been hardened off. These plants are robust and resistant, and will also cope with slightly warmer or very shady positions as well as with low humidity.
Care: Water plentifully during the summer; otherwise keep medium moist. This fern will forgive the occasional slight drying out of the compost. Give weak doses of fertilizer weekly from early spring to early fall. These plants love mild rain showers or misting. Repot every one to two years in the spring.
Propagation: From

spores or division.
Pests, diseases: Rare; scale insects or mealy bugs if the position is too warm and the air too dry.
My tip: An extremely undemanding fern with respect to position and care and, therefore, highly recommended for the beginner.

The hairy rhizomes of *Davallia* will creep along the edge of the pot or along an epiphyte trunk.

Davallia trichomanoides will flourish in a hanging container.

Davallia
Hare's foot fern

This small fern, with its finely partitioned fronds, is so pretty that it really merits wider distribution as an indoor plant. The usually tripartite feathered leaves form at intervals along the thick, above-ground rhizomes. Its densely distributed, yellowish, reddish-brown or white scales give it a woolly or hairy appearance which has given rise to the common name of hare's foot fern. The longish, urn-shaped spore capsules form at the ends of the lateral veins. Although the genus encompasses about 40 species, the species most commonly found in nurseries is *Davallia tricomanoides*. Other attractive species, such as *Davallia fejeensis*, *Davallia mariesii*, or *Davallia canariensis* are mostly found in botanical collections.

Family: *Davalliaceae*.
Origin: Temperate, sub-tropical but mostly tropical regions of Africa, Asia, Australia and Polynesia. Usually in trees and on mossy rocks. *Davallia canariensis* on the Canary Islands, Portugal, Spain, and Morocco.
Position: Bright to semi-shady, no sunlight. During the summer 68° F (20° C); in winter 54-59° F (12-15° C). *Davallia canariensis* will cope with lower temperatures. All species love high humidity.
Care: Always keep evenly moist. Do not let dry out. Avoid waterlogging. Give weak doses of fertilizer every four weeks from early spring to early fall. *Davallia* do well in the high humidity found in a glass case. Mist over often indoors. Only repot if necessary in the spring. Do not cover creeping rhizomes with compost. Use pots that are not too large and loose, well-drained compost (orchid compost, for example).
Propagation: From division or rhizome cuttings. Sowing spores is complicated. In specialty nurseries, propagation is carried out from tissue culture.
Pests, diseases: The rhizomes will decay if the compost is too moist, particularly in winter.
Warning: The fronds of certain species contain toxic cyanogenic glycosides.

Didymochlaena likes shade.

Doryopteris pedata.

Didymochlaena

Only one species is known of this fern which has shiny, dark green to bronze green fronds. This is *Didymochlaena truncatula*. The plant usually produces two-fold feathered fronds that are pink to reddish when they shoot and can attain a length of up to 28 in (70 cm) in cultivation. In its natural habitat the plant forms an approximately 16 in (40 cm) tall, thick stem when it is old.
Family: Aspidiaceae.
Origin: Grows terrestrially in tropical rain forests.
Position: Semi-shady to shady. During the summer about 68° F (20° C),
during the winter, 57-64° F (14-18° C) will be sufficient. High humidity is required.
Care: Keep evenly moist. In winter, when temperatures are lower, water less. Do not let the compost dry out as the fern will drop its fronds. Give weak doses of fertilizer every two weeks from early spring to early fall. Mist frequently, particularly when the plant is forming shoots. Repot once a year in the spring.
Propagation: From spores or division.
Pests, diseases: None known.
My tip: Suitable for north-facing windows.

Doryopteris

This fern has wide, lobed leaves on wiry stems. The sterile fronds have shorter stalks and broader partial surfaces, the fertile ones longer stems and narrower segments. The spore capsules form stripes along the edges of the leaves. Of the 35 species only *Doryopteris pedata* is readily available from nurseries. Breeder buds (bulbils) grow on the leaves where the leaf emerges from the stalk. These develop into tiny plantlets.
Family: Sinopteridaceae.
Origin: In all tropical countries; *Doryopteris pedata* only in tropical
America. Terrestrial fern, grows on rocks.
Position: Bright to semi-shady, no sunlight. The same indoor temperature all year round. Not below 61° F (16° C) during the winter.
Care: Keep evenly moist In winter water less when temperatures are low. Sensitive to waterlogging Give low doses of fertilize every four weeks from early spring to early fall. Make sure ventilation is good. Repot in spring if necessary.
Propagation: From spores and offset plantlets.
Pests, diseases: None known.

The curled-up young frond resembles a bishop's crozier.

During their development the frond tips unfurl and the young leaves begin to open. Finally, the young frond will stretch upward.

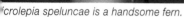

crolepia speluncae is a handsome fern.

icrolepia

e 45 species of this nus include large, posing ferns, some of ich are suitable for owing indoors. The gen- ally fine feathering of the ves makes this a aceful plant but, often, ey can be kept as pot nts for only one or two ars as they become too ge for small rooms.

Microlepia speluncae the only species com- only obtainable from rseries. Its light green, ft, often slightly droop- g fronds emerge at ort intervals from the eping rhizome. They n attain lengths of up to in (2 m) in their natural habitat but will grow to only half that length indoors. The triangular fronds have stalks about 20 in (50 cm) long, are partitioned three or four times and are slightly hairy.

● *Microlepia strigosa* possesses upright to over- hanging, two- or three-fold fronds and remains a little smaller.

● *Microlepia platyphylla* looks quite different from the other species described above due to its more coarsely feathered, bluish-green, shiny fronds. In this genus the spore clusters develop along the edges of the leaves and at the ends of the lateral veins.

Family: *Dennstaedtiaceae.*
Origin: These are terres- trial ferns from the tropics of Africa and Asia where they often grow on the shady floors of forests or along the banks of rivers. *Microlepia speluncae* occurs in all tropical and subtropical countries, even along the edges of forests.
Position: Bright to semi- shady, no direct sunlight. Even room temperature all year round; in winter a lit- tle cooler (to 59° F/15° C). This plant loves high humidity.
Care: Water plentifully in summer; keep it a little drier during the winter. Fertilize weekly from the first month of spring to the first month of fall. Mist frequently. Repot every spring as this fern develops a vigorous root system.
Propagation: From spores or division.
Pests, diseases: Scale insects.
My tip: Can be planted in a conservatory as a com- panion plant for smaller ferns.

A group of various Nephrolepis species.

Nephrolepis exaltata "Corditas."

Nephrolepis

With its short-stalked, elegantly drooping fronds, this plant is the archetypal fern. About 30 species are distributed throughout the tropics and subtropics

Nephrolepis exaltata "Verona Lace."

all over the world where they flourish so abundantly that they are considered as weeds in gardens. Their great proliferation of shoots means that they can spread rapidly and will soon cover the entire surface of a pot. The fronds of some species may grow 40 in (1 m) long. The pure species possess single-feathered fronds. The individual leaflets are more or less curled or wavy, the edges serrated or lobed. The spores develop in kidney-shaped clusters at the ends of the lateral veins.

The fronds are ideally suited for use as greenery in flower arrangements or bouquets.

● Nephrolepis exaltata is the species most often offered for sale, and with the most varieties. The oldest variety, which is still available today, was discovered in America in 1870 and became famous under the name "Bostoniensis" or simply as "Boston fern." Many other varieties have derived from this early ancestor. There are now many different types, with varying shades of green, single- or multi-feathered fronds and different rates of growth. Some more compact varieties are "Boston Dwarf," with upright growth, "Maassii" with relatively smooth

fronds, or "Teddy Junior" with wavy fronds. "Rooseveltii," on the other hand, grows large and spreading. "Little Linda," and "Veronica Lace" are small, fine, multi-feathered densely growing types.

● Nephrolepis cordifolia possesses stiffer, dark green fronds that grow up to 24 in (60 cm) long but are only about 2 in (5 cm wide.

A special feature of this species is the underground tubers that appear at the ends of the shoots. The varieties most often for sale are usually "Compacta," which remains small, or "Plumosa," the feathery leaves of which are

Nephrolepis cordifolia "Duffii" has narrow, light green fronds.

Many varieties of ferns show different degrees of feathering on one frond. The fronds of Nephrolepis cordifolia "Plumosa" are divided again in their outer sections.

vided in their outer alves. The unusual variy "Duffii" has very narw fronds with almost und, very light-colored aflets for this species.

Nephrolepis biserrata a very vigorously growg species with fronds at may grow up to 40 in m) long when cultivat- d. The frond ends of the riety "Furcans" (somenes also grouped under ephrolepis falcata) are rked several times.

amily: Nephrolepidaceae rigin: Nephrolepis altata and Nephrolepis serrata are distributed roughout the tropical gions of the world. ephrolepis cordifolia curs in tropical Asia and New Zealand. Nephrolepis may grow terrestrially but also as an epiphyte.

Position: Bright to semishady. No direct sunlight but it will cope with more light than many other ferns. Stable room temperature all year round; in winter not below 64° F (18° C). This plant loves high humidity.

Care: Constant, even humidity is particularly important for this fern. Do not let it dry out but avoid waterlogging! The best way to fulfil these requirements is by using clay peg irrigation (see p. 18). Nephrolepis cordifolia can cope with a little more dryness. Give a weak dose of fertilizer every two weeks from the first month of spring to the first month of fall. Mist over frequently. Varieties that grow vigorously should be repotted every year; others only when necessary in the spring.

Propagation: From rhizomes or division; the species also from spores. In the case of Nephrolepis cordifolia, you may also propagate from tubers with a section of the rhizome. Nephrolepis exaltata is usually propagated by tissue culture in specialty nurseries as many varieties do not produce spores.

Pests, diseases: Spider mites are encouraged by too low humidity. Also Diptera, Sciaridae. Pale green feathers that are finally shed indicate a rootstock that is too wet or too dry or a position that is too dark.

In Pellaea falcata the sporangia appear along the edges of the fronds to create an interesting pattern that contrasts with the leaf veins.

A group of Pellaea falcata and Didymochlaena truncatula (front left).

Pellaea
button fern

The button fern belongs among a group of plants that would not at first glance be counted among ferns. Spores form in strips along the leaf edges.

● Pellaea rotundifolia is the pot plant most often offered for sale out of all the 80 species. It possesses very dark, single-feathered fronds with circular, leathery leaflets that look like a string of pearls on the scaly, dark brown leaf ribs. The plant will grow to about 8 in (20 cm) tall and is relatively robust.

● Pellaea falcata is a simple species with longish-oval feathery leaves.
● Pellaea viridis has single to tripinnate, 24-in (60-cm) long fronds with longish triangular feathers and black leaf ribs.
Family: Sinopteridaceae.
Origin: Pellaea rotundifolia originates from New Zealand and from Norfolk Island; Pellaea falcata from southern Asia, Australia, Tasmania, and New Zealand; Pellaea viridis from South Africa, Madagascar, and the Mascarene Islands. Button ferns are terrestrial or rock-dwelling plants, usually found growing in temperate to subtropical

regions and also often found in dry regions.
Position: Bright to semi-shady, no direct sunlight. The plants love a cool, fresh place, like a stair-way. In the winter the temperature may sink as low as 54° F (12° C). Pellaea viridis requires slightly warmer temperatures.
Care: Always keep it just slightly moist. During the winter when the temperatures are lower, water sparingly but still do not let the plant dry out. Give weak doses of fertilizer every four weeks from the first month of spring to the first month of fall. Ensure there is good ventilation. Only repot in the

spring if necessary. Use nutrient-poor compost (for example, seeding compost) and do not use pots that are too large.
Propagation: From spores or division. Pellaea rotundifolia is propagated in specialty nurseries through tissue culture.
Pests, diseases: Scale insects.
My tip: Pellaea rotundifolia will cope with dry indoor air.

Phlebodium

best known of the ten
cies is *Phlebodium
eum*. It has deeply
ented fronds and
sh, long-stalked
ves. Mature specimens
grow to more than
in (1 m) in height. The
cies suffix *aureum*
(den) is explained by
creeping, above-
und rhizomes which
covered in round, yel-
clusters of spores.
variety "Maidaianum"
wavy leaf edges and
ws to only about 30 in
cm) tall. "Cristatum"
curly leaf tips.
nily: *Polypodiaceae.*
gin: Tropical to sub-
pical America.
sition: Only in a bright
sition will the leaves
w their characteristic
active coloring. Even
m temperature all year
nd; at least 61° F
° C) during the winter.
cope with dryish air.
re: Water plentifully
ing the summer but
id waterlogging. Drier
ing the winter. Give
ak doses of fertilizer
ry two weeks from the
t month of spring until
first month of fall.
casionally mist. Repot
he spring if required.
not cover the
zomes.
pagation: From
res and rhizome
ision.
sts, diseases: Scale
ects.

Phlebodium requires enough room for undisturbed development.

A splendid specimen of Platycerium bifurcatum.

Platycerium
staghorn fern

The popularity of this exotic plant is not without good reason as its unique shape draws attention and large specimens can prove an eye-catching feature. The undemanding character of these plants, which do not mind if you occasionally forget to water them, and their imperviousness to warm, dry, centrally heated air are additional welcome characteristics.

Platycerium is well adapted to its life as an epiphyte in trees. First of all, it produces sterile, often smooth-edged leaves that curl backward to lie close to the trunk or branch. These are barren leaves. The oldest of these leaves gradually dry up and then remain for a long time as brown, paper-like layers underneath newly forming leaves. This creates a kind of funnel in which humus and water are caught. The fertile leaves grow upright or droop from this rosette. They are strong, green or grayish-green, and, depending on the species, more or less deeply lobed. A whitish-gray film protects them from losing too much water through evaporation. The spores are unusual in that, depending on the species, they form as large, dark brown to black patches either on the tips of the leaves (*Platycerium bifurcatum*) or on the surface of the leaf just below a fork (*Platycerium grande*).

The genus comprises seventeen species of which *Platycerium bifurcatum*, with some varieties, is usually the one most often offered for sale in garden centers and nurseries.

● *Platycerium bifurcatum* merits the name staghorn fern because of its multiple-lobed fertile leaves. This is a very variable species which forms huge colonies in its natural habitat.

Of all the other species, a few can sometimes be viewed in botanical collections. They appear in an interesting range of shapes, especially in the design of their leaves.

● *Platycerium grande* is sometimes offered for sale. It has very large, upright leaves with lobes around the edges.

● *Platycerium superbum* resembles *Platycerium grande* and also forms large individual specimens

● *Platycerium angolense* has undivided fertile leaves and barren leaves with wavy edges.

● *Platycerium coronarium* has deeply indented 120-in (3-m) long fertile leaves that hang down like straps.

● *Platycerium madagascariense* forms an interesting net-like pattern on its barren leaves which have protruding leaf veins. This species requires cooler temperatures.

Family: Polypodiaceae.
Origin: Most species originate from the tropical regions of southern China to upper India, Malaysia, Indonesia, the Philippines, New Zealand, and Australia. Individual species are also to be found in tropical Africa, Madagascar, the Mascarene Islands, the Comoros Islands, and the Seychelles, as well as in Peru and Bolivia. They usually grow in moist, warm rain forests as epiphytes on tree trunks and in the forks of branches among rocks.
Position: Bright to semi shady. Even temperature

...ore clusters on the frond tips of Platycerium bifurcatum.

Platycerium grande produces barren leaves.

year round; during the ...ytime 64-77° F (18-...° C). Temperatures may ...k as low as 59° F ...5° C) during the night. ...ese plants prefer ...edium humidity but will ...so cope with drier air. **...re:** Water only sparingly, ...rticularly in slightly ...oler positions and in ...nter, but never let them ...y out completely. It is a ...od idea to immerse ...em in water every one ...two weeks. ...aterlogging is lethal! ...d low doses of fertilizer ...the water used for ...atering or immersing ...ery two weeks from the ...st month of spring to ...e first month of fall. Do ...t spray. On no account

remove any dead barren leaves. The wax layer on the surface of the leaves should never be damaged as it protects the fern from excessive evapora- tion. These plants feel most comfortable growing on pieces of bark or on epiphyte trunks but you can also plant them in little wooden baskets. If *Platycerium* are grown in pots, they should only be repotted when absolutely necessary. Choose a loose compost (for exam- ple, orchid compost) and containers that are not too large.

Propagation: From spores or by division. *Platycerium bifurcatum* is often propagated through

tissue culture in specialty nurseries.

Pests, diseases: Scale insects. Note that *Platycerium* ferns do not react well to most plant protection agents.

My tip: If you decide to fertilize your *Platycerium* while immersing it in water, you can use the excess fertilizer solution for watering other ferns or indoor plants afterward. This saves on fertilizer and is better for the environment.

Many Polypodium species produce attractive creeping rhizomes. Polypodium lucidum rhizomes are shiny green with black markings. Depending on the size of the plant, the fronds can grow over 40 in (1 m) long and the rhizomes to ¾-1¼ in (2-3 cm) thick.

Polypodium polycarpon "Grandiceps."

Polypodium

This large, variable genus is well known as an ornamental outdoor fern. Some species are indigenous to Europe, such as *Polypodium vulgare* whose roots were often used as a planting medium for orchids and epiphytes years ago. Most of the species, however, are accustomed to warm climates and will only flourish indoors in a temperate climate. Unfortunately, they are not often found for sale in garden centers or nurseries. These plants possess creeping rhizomes and feathered or undivided leaves. The mostly circular spore clusters appear in rows parallel to the central ribs. They are protected by hairs. Often, the leaves are slightly depressed wherever the spores are situated. Usually slow-growing.

● *Polypodium polycarpon* and its varieties are most common. They have narrow, undivided, leathery, up to 20-in (50-cm) long leaves which, in some varieties, may be dentate or forked at the tip as in "Grandiceps."

● *Polypodium longifolium* has very narrow, long leaves that are ¾ in (2 cm) wide and 24 in (60 cm) long.

● *Polypodium lucidum* and *Polypodium scan-*dens are among the species with feathered leaves.

Family: *Polypodiaceae.*
Origin: Generally found in the tropics or subtropics. *Polypodium* grow as terrestrial or rock ferns but also as epiphytes.
Position: Bright to semi-shady, no sunlight. Even room temperatures all year round; may be cooler during the winter (down to 54° F/12° C). These plants prefer medium humidity.
Care: Keep evenly moist during the spring and summer months but avoid waterlogging. Water less during the winter. Give low doses of fertilizer weekly from the first month of spring to the first month of fall. Make sure ventilation is good. Usually these plants are grown as epiphytes but they can also be planted in pots. Make sure the compost is permeable and only repot if necessary during the spring.
Propagation: From division or spores.
Pests, diseases: Scale insects.

olystichum tsus-simense.

Unripe spore clusters on the under sides of fronds.

olystichum

olystichum are known
ainly as outdoor ferns in
orthern Europe.
olystichum munitum,
uch prized by florists,
elongs to this genus. It
as originally imported
om North America and
s fronds are used as
reenery with flower
rangements and
ouquets. It is almost
xclusively Polystichum
us-simense that is found
r sale as an indoor fern.
his small species took its
ame from a group of
apanese islands called
sushima. In diameter it is
oout 6-8 in (15-20 cm)
nd it grows to a height of
oout 12 in (30 cm). Its

leaves are oval, longish,
and bipinnate. The leaf
stalks have many dark
brown scales in their
lower sections and are
hairy farther up. The
round clusters of spores,
which have shield-shaped
veils, form two regular
rows between the edge of
the leaf and the central rib
of the leaf.
This fern has a particularly
attractive appearance due
to its dark green, leathery
fronds. It is, however, also
of interest because of its
preference for cooler
positions. It is even hardy
in regions that are warm
enough for grapevines to
grow, provided it is pro-
tected with a covering of
dead leaves.

Family: Aspidiaceae.
Origin: This genus is
distributed worldwide in
temperate to subtropical
regions. The plants grow
terrestrially, often in
mountainous forests and
along the banks of rivers.
Polystichum tsus-simense
originates from Korea,
Japan, China, and
Taiwan.
Position: Bright but not
sunny. This plant can
cope with cooler tempera-
tures between 54° F and
61° F (12° C and 16° C)
and even as low as 41° F
(5° C) during the night.
Care: Keep evenly moist
during the growth phase.
Water less during the winter but do not let it dry
out. Give low doses of

fertilizer weekly from the
first month of spring to
the first month of fall. With
its leathery leaves, this
fern can cope with drier
air but is also grateful for
the occasional misting.
Repot annually in the
spring.
Propagation: From divi-
sion or spores.
Pests, diseases: None
known.
My tip: *Polystichum tsus-
simense* is eminently suitable for bottle gardens
because of its small size.

Pteris quadriaurita "Tricolor."

Pteris cretica "Roewerii."

Pteris

The single or bipinnate fronds of this variable genus are often curled at the tips. The leaf stalks are smooth and thin, yellow, green, or brown.

● *Pteris cretica* is the species most often offered for sale. Its sterile young leaves have short stalks and broad feathers. Later on, upright fronds with narrower feathery leaves are formed, with spores appearing in a continuous line along their edges (except for at the tips of the feathers). The spore clusters are protected underneath the recurved leaf edges. There are green-leafed varieties, such as "Parkeri," "Roeweri," and "Wimsettii," and green and white striped varieties, such as "Albolineata" and "Mayi."

● *Pteris ensiformis* "Evergemiensis" produces very elegant small plants with green and white variegated leaves.

● *Pteris argyrea* has leaf fronds that shine silvery white at their bases.

● *Pteris quadriaurita* "Tricolor" has greenish-red fronds.

● *Pteris tremula* may grow to a height of over 40 in (1 m).

Family: *Pteridaceae.*
Origin: Tropics and subtropics, some species also in temperate regions.

Exclusively terrestrial ferns.

Position: Bright to semi-shady; green foliage species also shady, no sun. Green foliage types cool (59-64° F/15-18° C); variegated ones warmer (64-68° F/18-20° C); during the winter down to 37° F (3° C). Most of the species prefer high humidity.

Care: Always keep constantly moist. During the winter, water less in cooler positions but never let the ferns dry out. Give low doses of fertilizer weekly from the first month of spring to the first month of fall. Spray frequently. Repot annually during the spring.

Propagation: From spores or division.
Pests, diseases: Aphids on the young shoots.

A selection of Pteris species

Back row (from left to right): Pteris cretica "Mayi," Pteris cretica "Albolineata," Pteris fauriei; front row (from left to right): Pteris cretica "Parkeri," Pteris ensiformis "Evergemiensis," Pteris dentata "Stramina, Pteris fauriei.

Rarities

Actiniopteris australis

The fan-shaped, indented, dark green leaves of this dwarf fern are reminiscent of palms. It grows to about 8 in (20 cm) tall and is very suitable for bottle gardens. The spores are protected by the curled-up edges of the leaves.
Family: Actiniopteridaceae.
Origin: Tropical Africa and Asia.
Position: Shady to bright; room temperature; high humidity.
Care: Water plentifully during spring and summer but avoid waterlogging. During the winter, when the temperatures are lower, water less frequently. Even moisture is very important for this fern. Do not let it dry out or the fronds will turn silvery gray and will not recover again. Fertilize every four weeks.

The climbing fern, Lygodium.

The golden fern, Pityrogramma.

Lygodium

Lygodium japonicum can climb up to over 50 ft (15 m) high in its natural habitat, using its long, wiry stalks and the stems of its leaves. It can be used as a "green tapestry" in a room. The spores develop on fine lobes along the edge of the fertile fronds.
Family: Lygodiaceae.
Origin: Tropics and subtropics.
Position: Bright to semi-shady. During the daytime 64-68° F (18-20° C); during the night around 61° F (16° C). Loves high humidity.
Care: Keep evenly moist all the time. Fertilize every four weeks. Spray frequently. Requires sticks, twines, or wires as a climbing aid.

Actiniopteris australis is graceful but a little difficult to grow.

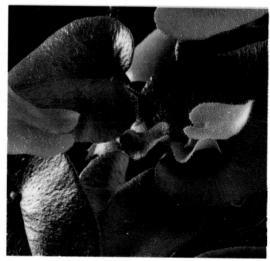

Hemionitis arifolia with breeder plantlets.

A frond of Blechnum moorei bearing lines of spores.

Pityrogramma

Many species of this genus are characterized by a white, light yellow, or golden yellow floury film on the leaf under sides. The spores develop along the veins.
Family: Hemionitidaceae.
Origin: Mostly tropical America, also South Africa and the west African islands. Tendency to colonize dry positions.
Position: Bright. Temperatures around 59° F (15° C) are generally sufficient.
Care: Always keep just slightly moist. Avoid waterlogging! Fertilize every four weeks. Do not spray as this destroys the floury film.

Hemionitis arifolia

Tiny plantlets develop out of the bulbils (see photograph above right) on the heart-shaped leaves of this unusual dwarf fern. Spores form along the veins on the longer-stalked fertile leaves.
Family: Hemionitidaceae.
Origin: Tropical Asia.
Position: Bright to semi-shady; room temperature.
Care: Keep constantly slightly moist. Avoid waterlogging. Fertilize every four weeks. Only repot when necessary and do not use pots that are too large as this fern develops only a modest root system.

Blechnum moorei

Blechnum moorei from New Caledonia is an attractive, but very rarely obtainable fern species. Care is similar to that of other *Blechnum* species.

Arachniodes adiantiformis

This fern (see p. 22) is popular as greenery to accompany cut flowers but is rarely offered for sale as a pot plant. It is a resilient fern for cooler positions (daytime 59-64° F/ 15-18° C). At night and in winter 50° F (10° C) will suffice.
Warning: Spore-producing specimens of this fern can cause skin irritation and should be avoided by people with allergic reactions.

Plants related to ferns

Selaginella

The genus *Selaginella* does not belong among the genuine ferns but with the *Sellaginellaceae* (fern-like plants). This class developed its wide range of shapes and forms millions of years ago. As well as the 130 ft (40 m) tall scale and seal trees that belong in this class, and which dominated the forests of the carboniferous age, there were also some leafy species. It is quite astonishing to think that members of the genus *Sellaginella* (club mosses) still in existence today resemble plants that first developed about 350 million years ago.

Selaginella kraussiana.

Selaginella martensii "Watsoniana."

Of the approximately 700 known species, only two are indigenous to the Alps of central Europe; the others originate mostly from the tropics.

The shoots of club moss are usually branched in forks and covered in four rows of scale-like tiny leaves. In the case of species that grow in a creeping fashion, they soon form a green carpet. In many species, light-colored, leafless shoots emerge from the branching of the stalks. Roots will grow from these.

The spore-bearing leaflets of the club mosses form four-sided, terminal spikes. Each spore leaf carries only one spore capsule which is formed where the leaf emerges. Male sporangia with many minute spores and female ones with four large spores are produced and grow together on one spike. The development of both male and female cells begins before the spores have left their capsules. The genus is very variable. In addition to low-growing, prostrate types there are also upright or even climbing ones. Leaves appear in all shades from yellow to bright green and blue green. There are also white/green and yellow/green variegated types. Those most frequently found in garden centers and nurseries are *Selaginella apoda* and varieties of *Selaginella kraussiana*, as well as *Selaginella martensii*.

Selaginella martensii.

fall. Spray frequently.

Propagation: From branch tips that can be pinned down to compost or from division. Some species can be propagated from young plantlets that form on the leaves.

Pests, diseases: None known.

My tip: Club mosses are very suitable as an underplanting for larger ferns. Small species grow well in bottle gardens.

Club mosses can be grown as pot plants.

Selaginella apoda from North America is very low-growing and looks like a moss.

Selaginella kraussiana originates from tropical and southern Africa. It forms dense carpets with its prostrate, 12-in (30-cm) long branches.

Selaginella martensii (photograph above left), from Mexico, grows upright and is supported by strong roots. It can grow up to 12 in (30 cm) tall.

Selaginella gracilis comes from Polynesia. It can grow up to 36 in (90 cm) tall but still looks very dainty.

Selaginella willdenowii from tropical Asia can climb up to several feet (meters) using its protruding frond shoots. Blue-green fronds.

Family: Selaginellaceae.

Origin: Tropics, subtropics and temperate regions. Mostly in tropical rain forests, more rarely in dry regions.

Position: Most species offered for sale as indoor plants require shade or semi-shade, even temperatures all year round and high humidity. Protect from drafts.

A variety of Selaginella kraussiana.

Selaginella apoda.

Care: Keep evenly moist. Avoid waterlogging. Never let the rootstock dry out; the plants will not usually recover from this. Give low doses of fertilizer from the first month of spring to the first month of

Index

Numbers given in **bold** indicate illustrations.

Acknowledgements

The author, the photographer, and the publishers would like to thank the following for their help in procuring the plants used for the photographs:

P. W. Eveleens, Royal Eveleens, Aalsmeer, The Netherlands
Frans Didden, Royal Eveleens, Aalsmeer, The Netherlands
Bloemen Bart, Noordwijk, The Netherlands
Walburga Weiss, Furth, Germany
Andre Noack, Furth, Germany
Ruhe Varens, Amstelveen, The Netherlands
Michael Grille, Gartenbau Rothe, Berlin, Germany

Author's notes

This book deals with the care of indoor ferns. Some of the plants discussed are slightly toxic. In the plant descriptions (pp. 34-59) the keyword "Warning" gives information where there is any risk to health. Never eat any parts of these plants and make sure that children or domestic pets do not have access to them. Spore-producing plants sometimes possess skin-irritant properties. People with allergies should avoid these plants. Always follow the manufacturer's directions meticulously (and the recommendations on p. 30) when using plant protection agents. Always keep children and domestic pets well away when treating plants with any agents.

Cover photographs

Front cover: *Nephrolepis exaltata.*
Back cover: *Maidenhair fern (Adiantum raddianum).*

Photographic acknowledgments

Amberger-Ochsenbauer: p. 37 left top, 37 bottom left, 41 left, 41 right, 45 center, 45 right, 48 right, 51 left, 52 right, 53 right, 56 top left, 57 left, 58 bottom; Eisenbeiss: p. 5 bottom, 12, 32/33, 38 right, 62/63; Photoplant: p. 5 top; Stork: all other photos

This edition published 1996 by Landoll, Inc.
By arrangement with Merehurst Limited Ferry House, 51-57 Lacy Road, Putney, London SW15 1PR.
© 1992 Gräfe und Unzer GmbH, Munich

ISBN 1-56987-699-1

Text copyright ©
Merehurst Limited 1996
Translated by Astrid Mick
Edited by Lesley Young
Design and typesetting by
Paul Cooper Design